MW01127599

RELEASED!

OVERCOMING

SEXUAL TRAUMA

Paul G. Helton, Ph.D.

and

Katie Maurice

Copyright © 2016 Paul G. Helton, Ph.D. and Katie Maurice

All rights reserved.

ISBN: 10:1512209953

ISBN-13: 978-1512209952

Contents

Acknowledgements

First and foremost, I want to thank God for allowing me the continued opportunities to partner with people, like Katie, and many others in this journey of life. Their efforts to improve their lives and circumstances are a constant source of encouragement to me.

Many people are behind the scenes lending support in the production of this book. Katie and I are blessed to have so many people who stand behind us.

I give special thanks to my wife Dana for being a patient friend who has loved me unconditionally for all of our married life. My heart has been blessed by my three daughters Sarah, Emily, and Molly for the many hours they all spent proofing and editing the text. They constantly heard me say, "Read this and tell me what you think." All were patient and supportive.

Thanks to Dr. Ryan Fraser, my friend and colleague, for reviewing and giving suggestions on the manuscript. He was also gracious enough to write a book review.

Special thanks to Dr. C. J. Vires, Vice President of Academic Affairs at Freed-Hardeman University, who encourages professors, like me, to reach for greater heights of scholarly activity. His friendship and spiritual demeanor are a constant source of personal encouragement.

Many thanks to Holly Rowsey for her diligent work and the countless hours she spent in helping with layout, structure, and format of this book. Her work provided many suggestions, which served to enhance the end product.

Special thanks to Dr. Richard England and Taraleigh Stemler for their many hours of editing and patient feedback. Their contributions were invaluable.

My heartfelt thanks I extend to my dear mother, Betty Ann Belew Helton, for always believing in me. Although she has left this life for another, she still continues to be one of my loudest cheerleaders. Thanks to my father, Gene Helton, for breaking the cycle of his past to bring a better life to me and my siblings.

This project would never have been possible without the enduring courage of Katie Maurice. Her fortitude and sheer determination to survive continues to inspire. I am confident you will be blessed by reading her story of heartache and triumph. Thank you.

Paul G. Helton, Ph.D., LPC, MHSP

I would like to dedicate this book to anyone who feels like they have no hope, because living without hope is not living at all. I pray my story will be a tiny piercing light in your weary soul.

I want to thank my loving husband and wonderful children who were constantly by my side through the good and the bad.

Most of all, I would like to thank Dr. Helton who kept his promise and never gave up on me. You saved my life and because of you I'm more than just surviving.

Katie Maurice

Special Note: A workbook companion to this book is available entitled *Released! Overcoming Sexual Trauma Workbook,* by Dr. Paul Helton and Taraleigh Stemler. The

workbook is especially suited for groups, college classes, or individuals who wish to work through a reflective analysis of the components involving sexual trauma.

Foreword

Writing a book is never easy, especially when it is one born of incalculable pain. Many people dream or even plan to write a book "one day," and many others take the first steps of a healing journey of recovery from enormous atrocities. Few, though, actually complete either project. Katie Maurice has persevered to do both.

Released! is a compelling story - heartbreaking and difficult to read, especially for someone who also experienced years of sexual abuse. I found myself affected by the story on an unexpected, visceral level. I felt it in my throat and in my gut and as a halo of gloom that hung over me, unshakeable for several hours. I grew increasingly angry as I read, not just at Katie's primary perpetrators, but also even more with the so-called "helpers" who caused her further harm.

Katie's profound pain and fragility bleed through these pages. Through my 23+ years of personal recovery and professional work, I've heard thousands of stories, and by this point, rarely am I surprised. I'm still, though, regularly astounded by the evil in the world, especially as perpetrated by family members on innocent children. Katie's story of repeated sexual abuse in her home is sadly common.

As a professional counselor, I react strongly to the ignorance and inadequacies rampant in my field. Too many people had opportunity to see Katie's pain and intervene; yet they failed to notice or take action. The supposedly trained counselors from whom she sought help are more culpable. I almost came out of my chair when I read Katie's account of an early counselor who told her she must have consented to violent sexual abuse because her perpetrator was close to her age. Such witless inexperience is beyond uninformed; it's rashly irresponsible.

Worse, another counselor whom Katie saw briefly as a teenager molested, instead of helped her. I think *Released!* should be required reading for every counselor-in-training as the textbook example that contrasts unethical, abusive practice with compassionate, informed assistance.

By God's grace, Katie encountered a safe, well-trained helper in Dr. Paul Helton, who was instrumental in Katie's release from her dungeon of self-hatred and shame. During the early months of their work together, Dr. Helton did much more than merely sit in silence when Katie was too bound up to speak or even look at him. He offered a steady, attuned presence she had never experienced, and that therapeutic connection developed the safe space where she could begin to unshackle her chains. Dr. Helton's instructive commentary on Katie's journey adds a clinical depth to the book. His personal commitment to her healing process, as evidenced by his willingness to receive additional training in EMDR to provide relief from her traumatic memories, is exemplary.

In the end, I was left wanting *more* – more about Katie's remarkable resilience and her painful path of release. More about Dr. Helton's patient progress and the skills that facilitated Katie's growth. More about her burgeoning trust in a God who was with her always and rejoices today in her release.

I am honored to be a fair witness to the truth of Katie's moving story. For too long, she was wounded repeatedly by those who overtly hurt her or who had no clue how to help her, until she came to blame herself and believe that she deserved her plight. Publishing *Released!* is Katie's resounding NO! to that belief and YES! to freedom.

All who read Katie's story, whether abuse survivor or those who seek to help them, will benefit from her amazing work.

Marnie C. Ferree, M.A., LMFT

Marnie C. Ferree is the director of Bethesda Workshops in Nashville, TN. She is the author of *No Stones – Women Redeemed From Sexual Addiction* and the editor of *Making Advances – A Comprehensive Guide for Treating Female Sex and Love Addicts.* You can learn more about her work at: http://www.bethesdaworkshops.org

Chapter 1

The Beginning Of The End

What you are about to read is a true story. It is a story of one of my clients who, for anonymity's sake, we will call Katie Maurice. In all my years as a therapist I have known many enduring, brave, bold, and resilient human beings, but none more so than Katie. Throughout this book a story will unfold that will allow you to know of her struggle to survive some of the most severe environments of sexual trauma I have ever encountered and treated. Her story needs to be heard and shared. For many survivors, their stories are held within themselves and never reach the hearts of compassionate hearers. Katie has made the decision to tell her story. It comes from deep within her spirit. You will notice that in various parts there will be italicized words. Those are my thoughts as her therapist. Katie's words will be in regular font.

Millions of people can identify with the facts that make up her life, which consists of immense suffering and pain that no human should ever have to bear. What makes this story moving is that not only did she survive, but she is moving forward with her life. Unfortunately, not everyone who experiences such trauma survives and lives to fight another day. Each year, worldwide, many helpless victims will take their lives in an effort to quiet the unrest contained in their spirits.

One study published in the <u>Journal of Suicide and Life Threatening Behavior,</u> analyzes data from a Youth and Risk Behavior Survey that sampled more than 31,000 teenagers in 2009 and 2011. The research continues a preliminary study from 2011 that found similar results using a smaller sample of teens.

The poll-surveyed students ages 14 to 18 and examined whether sexual assault and struggles with weight influenced suicide attempts within a year of the survey.

For boys, highlights of the study include:

- *3.5 percent of healthy-weight males with no sexual assault history attempted suicide.*
- *33.2 percent of healthy-weight males with sexual assault history attempted suicide. This can be attributed to stigma, shame, possible gender role conflict if the attacker was male, and the lack of an open support system.*
- *Weight alone is not a significant factor in suicide attempts for males. Only 3.9 percent of overweight males with no sexual assault history attempted suicide.*
- *33 percent of males who were both overweight and had a history of sexual assault attempted suicide.*

For girls, significant findings include:

- *5.8 percent of healthy-weight females with no sexual assault history attempted suicide.*
- *27.1 percent of healthy-weight girls with a history of sexual assault attempted suicide.*
- *8.2 percent of overweight girls with no sexual assault history attempted suicide.*

Both factors did not increase suicide rate: 26.6 percent of overweight girls with sexual assault histories attempted suicide. (http://www.futurity.org/sexually-assault-boys-suicide-891742/). Far and away, the suicide statistics are weighted against those who have suffered sexual trauma at the hands of perpetrators.

Although though Katie attempted suicide once, she was unsuccessful. She has told me that thinking about dying dominated so much of her daily thinking. Her story is one of ultimate survival that will bless, inspire, and encourage all who read the account of how her life has made the turn for which so many survivors long.

As her therapist, I have been honored to be part of Katie's recovery. Our sessions, as we have both agreed, were often as challenging for one as they were for the other. At times neither she nor I could find the words to adequately express what we were thinking and feeling. Never have I sat through more agonizing and difficult sessions. Often the sessions would last four hours with Katie only speaking for about 20 minutes and sitting in silence the rest of the time. She once told me, "When you ask me a question, it's like you've thrown a bomb into my mind, and it goes into a million pieces." Katie had tremendous difficulty finding verbal expression within such a fractured mind. This was the reason for so much of her silence in our sessions. Katie was searching for the words and was overwhelmed with anxiety by the trauma of her memories.

A word to those who might wonder, "Why does a person have so much difficulty verbalizing their traumas?" This is where the field of neuroscience assists the counselor who is trying to help trauma victims. When a client is asked to explain a specific trauma, the mind can and oftentimes does go into a high state of alert. Most "talk therapy" sessions are geared toward tapping into the client's pre-frontal cortex. This is the part of the brain that does the executive decision-making and is highly aware of its surroundings.

When a client is asked to explain traumatic events, they often shift into the "fight, flight or freeze" to a part of their brain, namely the amygdala, which activates the limbic system. When the limbic system is activated through the Autonomic Nervous System by way of the Sympathetic Nervous System, the client's language systems can shut down. The two primary areas of the brain responsible for language comprehension and production are Broca's area and Wernicke's area.

In 1861, Paul Broca treated a patient who had been mute for 30 years. Only five days later, the patient died. Dr. Broca performed an autopsy and found a lesion in the left frontal cortex. In the years that followed, he examined many patients with language impairments. In almost all cases, they had significant damage to the same area of the brain. Broca's area is involved in speech production and language comprehension. Wernicke's area was first discovered in 1874 by the German neurologist Carl Wernicke. This area of the brain is responsible for comprehension of speech sounds.

As a person's brain activates the Limbic System, the pre-frontal activity slows down and can inhibit the patient's ability to speak. This is especially true for patients suffering from Post-Traumatic Stress Disorder who can be triggered into a PTSD flashback. Clinicians often describe a PTSD flashback in the following way: "When the past becomes present." Now, imagine asking a client to describe a rape, torture, or some other terrifying event. If their past becomes their present, the limbic system will go into hyper-drive and dominate the alarm systems in their body and shut the language centers down.

This was exactly what was happening with Katie. Just asking her to recall traumatic details would send her into a PTSD flashback and she could not verbalize the details. The language centers of her brain were going "offline" and being overcome by her limbic system arousal. This accounts for why she had such difficulty speaking while she was overcome by the vivid mental memories.

For those helpers, whether it be a psychiatrist, nurse practitioner, licensed clinical social worker, licensed professional counselor, or licensed psychologist, may I suggest that you add

EMDR to your list of treatment options. In my experience, far too many helpers are using methods that re-traumatize the patient. Let me be clear on this point: I do not believe these helpers are intentionally traumatizing their clients. Most helpers are kind-hearted, loving people who genuinely want to partner with individuals for the expressed purpose of helping them toward growth and becoming all of which they are capable. With that said, I would encourage clinicians not to enter a counseling relationship with trauma clients without the necessary training in effective trauma modalities. To do otherwise would be an injustice to one's clients.

Had I not been willing to seek additional training to assist Katie, I would have made the decision to refer her to another professional that was more thoroughly trained in treatment of complex PTSD. As I had developed a therapeutic relationship and secured a measure of Katie's trust, I was more than willing to seek out the necessary training to help her move forward toward recovery.

Slowly, Katie is reclaiming her life. Although her struggles are far from over, she is learning to become a more integrated person and is experiencing greater feelings of normalcy and hope. It's as if she has been given a new lease on life. For so long, she was "stuck" in the vicious cycle of believing that nothing could be done to help her, no matter how hard she might try. Imagine for a moment that you are trapped in a waking nightmare and have no hopes of emerging as a whole person. That's where Katie was when I first met her. I did not realize how fragile a hold she had on life. I viewed her as another client who needed my help. She viewed me as her last hope for life. Going into the process held many unexpected twists and turns for me. What a journey it has been for both of us!

Katie has helped me to be more aware that, although a person may be functioning, life may not be fulfilling and hopeful. She was attending church, going shopping, being a wife, and being a mother to her children. From my perspective, she was doing well and was just a bit introverted. Working with her has helped me become a more compassionate helper to the hurting. A functioning person does not necessarily mean a "living" person. Most of her life, Katie wished for death, regardless of her circumstances.

Her story is one of the most resilient you will ever read. When I asked Katie why she would want to write about her pain and suffering, she responded by saying, "I want to give victims hope." For those who have been abused, she and I trust that as you read her story, hope will begin to emerge in your heart just like it has in Katie's spirit.

For those who have not suffered from abuse, we hope that you will use this material to encourage others who are searching for answers to their suffering and help them seek help for their pain. No one has to be forever trapped by the tormenting memories of trauma. Help is available. So, ask questions and consider credentials before choosing a therapist. Being more *informed will allow those who are seeking help to make more effective decisions before dealing with their pain-filled pasts. There is hope in your future!*

My first encounter with Katie came at her request. "I want to talk with you about prayer and forgiveness," she told me. It sounded like a reasonable request. Little did I know, I was about to embark on one of the most difficult journeys of my professional career. To be honest, I was blindsided by what came next.

Once seated in my office, Katie began to talk in general terms about not being able to forgive some family members for wrongs they had committed. As our conversation progressed, I asked what I thought to be a logical question: "How have you been wronged?" Unwilling to give specific answers, she proceeded to share with me the details of her unsuccessful experiences with at least four counselors, her suicide attempt, the loss of pleasure in normal life events, and her self-harming behaviors, like cutting. There was plenty of information about the aftershock, but nothing about how she had been wronged.

Any time I would ask for details of her past, Katie's demeanor would instantly change in a drastic manner. Up to that point in my life, I had never seen a client respond to questions in such a way. Her head would drop, her hair would fall forward so that her face was not visible, and she would become completely silent and unresponsive. This was my first experience with what I believed was severe dissociative behavior. Later, I will discuss a more formal diagnosis.

Whatever had been done to her created a deafening internal silence, which could not find its way from her mind through her mouth, so that it could be verbally expressed. She was completely unable to respond.

Finally, after several unsuccessful attempts at securing any specific details from Katie, she asked me a question: "Can I just write it down and let you read it?" "Absolutely," I responded. As we concluded, we agreed to enter a professional counseling relationship. I was to be her fifth counselor. Our journey toward heartache and healing was just beginning.

Let me share part of a letter Katie sent to me early on in the therapy process:

"When you don't recognize your emotions for a long time, they become hard to pinpoint. It is almost like they are a mystery. Most of the time I still feel blank, but sometimes I feel different. I feel like there is a spark of happiness or my heart feels less heavy. Sometimes it feels really heavy, like I have sunk to the bottom of the sea, and it is dark and lonely. Half of the time I have no clue what I am feeling, like maybe I need to get out my old chart with all the lists of feelings with the corresponding faces, and I still wouldn't be able to figure it out."

The letter you just read doesn't even begin to convey the shell of a person I saw sitting across from me in my office. One look into her face revealed a deep emptiness. I had seen this look before. It meant unspeakable pain and suffering. Katie literally would not be able to verbalize her trauma. She suffered from the aftershock of attachment issues, abandonment, torture, rape, sodomy, and bondage. All this suffering came from the hands of the people who were supposed to love, care for, and protect her, as well as model the appropriate behaviors of how to be successful in life. The suffering came to her from the last place one could have imagined: her family.

The word "family" for Katie was never a pleasant word. It represented everything that would lead to her immense depression, loss of identity, insecurities, and inability to ask for basic needs in her life. For her, the very word "family" came to represent reckless abandonment. If she had been left to fend for herself, that would certainly have been deplorable. Perhaps worse than being left alone, she was descended upon like prey to be stalked and attacked by a pack of lions. She was the youngest, the weakest, and the easiest target for those who had set out to steal her identity and voice as a human being. Instead of protecting her, they acted on their lusts and desires. Her story shows that with persistence, determination, hard work, and unwillingness to quit, a person can overcome life's greatest difficulties.

As easy as it would have been for her family's actions to break her spirit, she continued to fight to survive. She fought, with little to no help, to survive their constant attacks on her person. To defend herself, she chose a technique over time that ultimately served to protect. She sought invisibility. She chose *not to interact with people. She became a shadow in a crowd, keeping quiet so as to go unnoticed. She found ways to pretend so she wouldn't feel. She also depersonalized herself to avoid the intensity of constant suffering.*

She found the way that led to "the room" where she and she alone could hide. Deep within her was, as she put it, "the white room" of protection, with no people to touch her, inflict pain, or notice her. Interestingly, she would describe it to me as a room with no windows to see in or out, nor a door to enter or exit, with no fixtures of any kind. It was simply a white room with nothing in it but her. No way for her to leave and no way for anyone to get to her. Katie would use this empty room during times of abuse to propel herself beyond the immediate trauma that overwhelmed her mind with paralyzing fear. It was her escape. In time, Katie invited me to that room located deep within her heart, hidden from the sight of people.

From a clinical perspective, one can look up Post-traumatic Stress Disorder (PTSD) with dissociative symptoms in the Diagnostic and Statistical Manual of Mental Disorders, 5th edition, and consider the criterion for this disorder. Katie met all the criteria, so this was a proper diagnosis for her. Both dissociative symptoms of depersonalization and derealization were seen in most of our meetings for quite a long time.

When I first met with her and saw the symptoms of depersonalization and derealization, I found myself wanting to diagnose with Depersonalization-Derealization Disorder.

However, under criteria E, the DSM-5 states that, "The disturbance is not better explained by another mental disorder, such as...post-traumatic stress disorder..." (DSM-5 302). When considering the PTSD diagnosis, it became apparent that it was more suitable, especially since it allowed for dissociative symptoms specifiers (DSM-5 271-274).

Many trauma patients will demonstrate very similar symptoms to war veterans, particularly combat vets, who have experienced close fighting with all five senses engaged. The flashbacks are terrifying and often very difficult to manage in daily function. Such was the case with Katie. Daily life consisted of struggling to get through a day without having thoughts and flashbacks that were intrusive and impairing to her cognitive function. This created a life filled with significant distress in her mental processes and daily functioning.

A few days after our first meeting, Katie handed me a brown binder. It contained the painful details of her life and the subsequent sexual trauma that dominated her childhood and adolescence. Those details will be revealed to you as you continue to read. It goes like this...

Chapter 2

Loss of Innocence

From the outside, growing up in my family would probably have seemed normal to many people in typical American families. I grew up in a very conservative Christian home with a mother and father who I desperately wanted to love and cherish me. Unfortunately for me, that was not going to be a dream come true. My hopes of being treated with kindness, love and respect would never become a reality for me. For many reasons, which you will soon understand, my childhood consisted of constant attacks on my person, having my voice squelched, the destruction of my identity, and the complete loss of innocence.

I wish I could remember the good parts of my family life, but I really can't. You know, like family dinners, playing games, going to the park, being carefree. Not having a worry in the world. Being able to feel comfortable around my mother or feeling safe with my dad. Playing with siblings with no thought of them inflicting pain on me. In my daily life, things never felt normal. "Abnormal" is a better word to describe life in my family. My mental processes and behaviors were constantly alerted to danger. Looking back, I now realize that normal for me was always being afraid. Any fond memories are obscured and often buried by the intrusion of overwhelming fear and traumatic physical and sexual abuses.

My first memory of being sexually abused is when I was four years old. We lived in a house in the New England states. I remember my room very well. It was pink and white with a window seat, and I had a strawberry shortcake comforter. To an outsider, my room would have been considered normal. To me, my room was like a prison cell and a torture chamber, all mixed into one. Never have I recalled playing in my room like a normal kid.

On one occasion, my cousins were spending the night. One of my cousins was my best friend and was supposed to sleep in my room. She ended up getting the stomach flu and had to stay downstairs on the couch. My room was connected to my brother's room by a bathroom. Like most children, I was excited to have my cousins spend the night. After the kids, who were upstairs, had gone to bed, I got up to see what the other kids were doing. The adults were downstairs visiting. When I opened the door to my brother's room, I saw him and my cousin awake and it seemed to me that they were "playing." What I didn't know was that they were touching each other inappropriately. When they noticed that I was in the room, they said, "Come play with us." Naturally, I wanted to have fun and play, so I got under the covers. This was the first time they touched me in a sexual way. They were only a few years older than me and, looking back, I always told myself that maybe they were just curious. Now, I understand that my thinking was tainted by denial. They didn't physically hurt me that I remember. At that point, confusion began to take hold of a little girl's mind.

That is how it all started, as something I tended to think of as innocent curiosity. Now, as I see the reality of what was happening, it sickens me. The only innocent curiosity was that of a four-year-old little girl. To this day, I still am unsure as to how long my brother and cousin might have been engaged in this type of fondling behavior with one another. These events began to take on a vicious life of their own. My brother and cousin had chosen me as a new outlet for their sexual desires. Their abuse, which will be discussed in more detail later, would continue weekly for the next ten years of my life.

When I was left alone, I remember pretending a lot. Pretending to be a bird gave me the feeling of being able to fly away. Sometimes I would imagine myself as another person altogether. Many times, I would think of myself as one of my friends that I thought had a good life. These fantasies helped me to "get away" from my internal pain.

My parents would later tell me that I stopped wanting affection from them when I was four. I was already learning to dislike any form of physical contact. I just wanted to be left alone. There are so many times I wanted to know why my parents didn't wonder why I didn't like to be hugged or why I wouldn't say the words "I love you." What kept them from being aware of the circumstances of my captivity? Why? It shouldn't really matter to me because I can't change their responses, but it does matter. It never felt like my mom and dad cared what happened to me.

Someone asked me to explain why a child wouldn't want to say, "I love you." When a child is abused like Katie, a mental voice continues to play inside the child's head. At least, this is how Katie would explain it to me. It is like a constant video of people telling you that you are "not good," "bad," "sick," or that "it's all your fault." Over and over these negative messages begin to create neural circuitry in the brain that forms our identity. Literally, what "fires together, wires together." From a neurological perspective, the brain of the abused child is being built to replay negative messages that will serve to build a negative self-image, fueling low self-esteem.

These constant negative messages are part of the reason that "talk therapy" is so ineffective. Katie's brain was so saturated with negativity, that no matter how much I challenged her "irrational thoughts," she was unmoved emotionally and mentally. She fully embraced the concepts and beliefs that had been repeatedly told to her as a child. Remember that these statements had a great deal of sensory input that came with them. For example, while being raped, Katie was told that, "This is all your fault." Imagine being a small child and being told this while your body and brain were experiencing all the negative effects (e.g. bodily contact, sights, sounds, and even tastes) received by your senses. The negative cognitions are intensified by the sensory input of the trauma. This example serves to help us better understand "flashbacks." Even the smallest events or statements easily trigger many clients.

My brother, my two cousins, and I were always told by the adults that we had to play together. My other cousins were several years older or younger than us, so we were often forced together. Our parents would say, "go play," and we would be banished to the outdoors during daylight and good weather. Or, if it were nighttime or bad weather, the play would take place in the bedrooms. I have no recollection of an adult ever coming to "check in" on us.

Don't most adults periodically look in on the kids from time to time? This would have made a significant difference if my life had been permeated by actions from responsible adults. Sadly for me, no adult ever seemed to be aware of the actions of the children unless some behavior was staring them in the face. Even then the denial was so intense they refused to see all the warning signs. The adults seemed caught up with whatever they happened to be doing at the time.

One particular day, when I was about eight years old, our family went to visit some relatives who lived several hours away. It is hard to be certain of time and age because my memory tends to blur events together. We were at my cousins' house and we were told to play outside. I wasn't scared to play with them because they hadn't really hurt me until now. They wanted to play cops and robbers. They were the police officers and I was the "bad guy." They chased me, caught me, and took me to jail, which was a shed in the back yard. When they got me inside, they held me down and took off my clothes. They tied my hands with a jump rope. "We're tying you up because you are in jail," they said. The rope was green with purple handles.

After tying me up, they touched me and rubbed on me and put their fingers inside me. They thought it was funny when I cried and tried to get away. They also put different things inside me, like a screwdriver. Then, they untied me and let me put my clothes back on and sent me out to run and try to escape again. I tried to run as fast as I could, but they always caught me. I find it curious that it did not occur to me to run toward the house where the adults were. Now, I realize that my parents probably would not have believed me. At that point, neither of my parents was a source of comfort, strength, or safety to me. It was the first time my brother and cousin really hurt me; it was also the first time I learned to disappear.

It was almost like everything changed overnight. The casual touching produced confusion. These painful acts completely turned my mind inside out. The confusion turned into intense fear, terror, and horror. After this turning point, my life would be spent trying to make all those intrusive thoughts "go away." All my emotional energy was dedicated to the tasks of erasing the painful images and thoughts. Needless to say, I was not very successful.

That day, I experienced firsthand the cruelty of other human beings. Their depravity seemed to have no limits. It was as if what they were doing to hurt me gave them a strange sense of pleasure. It was like something inside of them snapped, and they became completely different people. Instead of feeling as though they were my family, I felt they were like hostile savages. It was as if they were criminals set on inflicting pain. That day marked the beginning of me losing myself. My individuality. My spirit. Me. Slowly but surely, I was vanishing.

By the time I was ten, my brother and cousin were forcing me to perform oral sex on them. The thing I hated the most was when they put objects inside of me. As they did this, I distinctly remember them laughing. Recalling specific things they said is very difficult. However, I do remember that they would talk back and forth to each other to "do more." But the thing I hated even more was when they made me do sexual things to them. It felt like the last bit of control I had was stripped away. My feelings of individuality were being replaced by the fact I came to accept: I was their "object." In my mind, all hope was gone. I resigned myself to believing that this was how my life would always be – that I would always be someone else's object to satisfy their sexual pleasure.

One of my earliest memories was when I started trying to find hiding places where I could feel safe. It started with when my dad started hurting me. I had two closets in my room, and I would hide in the right closet with my stuffed animals and blankets at night. I would fall asleep in there because I was afraid to be in my bed. It was about this time in my life that I started trying to disappear during the day. I would hide in the attic, in the woods, or under the bed. I would pretend that my little spaces were different worlds.

One time when I was around ten, I decided that I wanted a hiding place, so I could survive the summer of being home every day with my brother. Our family had a shed in the backyard that my family used as storage. It had a small loft that had no access to it. I found a way to climb onto the shelving and pull myself into the loft. I would take a flashlight and a book to read. I loved to get lost in books. I could pretend I was one of the characters and it would ease my worry. It seemed like the most perfect place ever, even if it was probably 100 degrees and stuffy. It was only a couple weeks before my brother found me there. He thought it was a great place too. It was a place that was shielded from view.

At first we would play like it was a fort. He had this way of making it seem like nothing bad would happen. We would play like we were best friends for a few days. Then, he would not want to play anymore. I can still smell the gasoline and rotted wood smell of the shed. I was scared not to do what he said because he would hurt me worse if I didn't cooperate with him. I only went back to the shed a couple times and he was always there waiting. So I stopped going there, but it didn't really matter. No matter how many times I tried to hide, they always found me.

Oftentimes at night, when they would make advances, I would try to pretend I was asleep or roll into a ball. It wasn't the best defense, but it was all I had. They still had their way with me. However, if they thought I was asleep, they would not force me to do things to them. Life for me was over.

To me the title of this chapter says it all: "Loss of Innocence." She came into this world as any other innocent baby girl, but soon thereafter, she would never enjoy a day of innocence. Katie has written a few pages here that do not do justice to the intensity of the depravity that she endured.

Imagine sitting with a person in four-hour therapy sessions for two years. Visualize week after week of listening to how evil other human beings can be toward one another. I heard stories of the most intense trials and tribulations of human suffering. You can imagine how long this book might be if Katie described the weekly abuse that lasted for years. What you've read in this chapter does not begin to unveil the depth of her tragedy. Hopefully, you have enough of the picture to imagine the enormity of her tragic circumstances.

It is important for me to stress the value of being a helper who can go the distance. Time was required to build the trust with Katie that would ultimately lead her to being more comfortable with sharing her pain, her struggles, and her desire for a better life. Trust is like building a bridge across the Grand Canyon. It's not built in a short period of time. My relationship with Katie has taken years to build. Patience is the number one ingredient for a successful recipe of integration toward a more wholehearted individual. Time is a gift that therapists can give to clients. Nothing can replace the therapist's patience during the passing of time.

Let me share part of a letter Katie wrote to me:

"I wish I could feel okay enough to cry. It almost hurts trying not to let the tears escape. It's like I can't let myself cry because I might not ever be able to stop the tears. Crying is too unpredictable. I want my mind to be free and not constantly wondering what will happen if I let go. I am terrified that if I let go, I will get stuck in my head and not be able to get back to reality. I hate feeling out of control."

This short excerpt gives a glimpse of the inner turmoil a victim wrestles with on a daily basis. Victims have endless thoughts of, "I'll never be free from this," or "Will I ever feel anything other than terror?" These thoughts plagued Katie's mind. In all of our therapy sessions, I have never seen Katie cry. However, she has told me on two occasions through texts that she was crying as she was thinking about her trauma. Read the next excerpt of another related letter:

I think this is one of the hardest things I have had to write. I have had this memory as long as I can remember. But, it is also the most vague memory I have. Sometimes I am watching the girl. Sometimes I am the girl. In the memory, I am three or four years old. At first the girl is in a bathtub. Someone picks her up and wraps her in a towel. He lays her on the bed. He touches her and puts his mouth on her. Then, she disappears.

Sometimes I would be floating above myself and could see what was happening. Other times I would daydream about playing outside by myself as an explorer. There were other times I would just stare at a spot up on the ceiling. I can't see his face. His hands seem huge and he had a beard because I can feel it. It's a really stupid memory, and I wish I could forget it.

A therapist can come alongside other people in their journeys and partner with them, empathize, seek to understand, listen to the heartache, and encourage them to see hope and a future. Asking clients what they would prefer to believe about themselves is a way to develop a "future template." This is one of the many techniques employed when using Eye Movement Desensitization and Reprocessing (EMDR). One of the greatest blessings of being a counselor is to attempt to lift another person's burden and somehow make it more bearable.

Allowing Katie to write her feelings was a much better way than to simply sit and wait for her to respond, which might take several minutes. Writing her thoughts was much easier than talking about them. Why? First, the client is usually journaling in an environment they feel safe. Second, it affords the client time to think through what they have written and rewrite if they choose. Many times, a client will come to therapy and be unprepared for the discussions. Finally, helping clients find "their voice" is essential to the healing process. In the beginning of her process, Katie made more headway with writing than talking. In time, as trust and confidence inside her grew, she would begin to feel more comfortable verbalizing her feelings.

I want to close this chapter with a part of Katie's journal where she reflects on her feelings related to her abuse.

For much of my life, I did not consider that what happened to me was abuse. For years, I believed that I was responsible in some way for the abuse that took place. When my second therapist told me I had been abused, it surprised me. It was true that what had happened to me was bad. But I thought it was my fault. In my mind, it couldn't be anyone else's fault because so many people were involved. That meant, in my mind, that the fault must be with me. I was bad. That's why bad things happened to me, because I'm bad.

When I got in school and had friends, I realized that they weren't abused. This gave me the feeling that since it wasn't happening to them, I must have done something wrong to bring the abuse on myself. My dad, brother, and cousins were constantly telling me that if anyone found out about what they were doing, I would get into trouble because it was my fault.

I think about what I tell the kids I work with— "...stay safe, say no, get away, and tell an adult." I guess part of the reason I didn't do anything was because I didn't feel unsafe. I felt like it was something that had to happen. There were a lot of reasons I didn't tell. I thought it was normal. It was something I grew up with. I had no choice. I felt scared that no one would believe me. I was afraid they would blame me, no one would love me anymore, and I would destroy our family. I was desperate for someone to find out, but I didn't want to be the one to tell. Sometimes I feel like I had reasons not to tell, but mostly I just feel like they are excuses.

Keep in mind that children, whether abused or not, have very little outside point of reference. To them, the actions of family members are considered normal. I recall a client who had suffered a great deal of abuse at the hands of her father. She recounted her story of sitting in her third grade class and having the thought of telling her teacher what her dad was doing. She said, "I looked around the class and thought to myself, 'Well, all these girls' fathers are doing the same things to them. So, it must be normal. Why should I tell?'" This is the result of having no reference point with which to weigh another's actions.

Other than interaction with her family, Katie had very little outside influence to gauge the morality of her family. This factor is significantly related to resigning herself to her plight and believing that the situation would always remain the same. Even now, in her marriage, Katie still feels the influence of those early traumatic events. Read an excerpt of one of her letters to me:

I feel embarrassed that my first sexual experiences were with my brother and cousins. While trying to go to sleep at night, I remember the feeling of stress, and thinking, "Will it be tonight?" I would almost feel relief when it happened. They would leave, and I could try to fall asleep knowing they probably were not coming back that night. Sometimes they might wait a day between episodes. The uncertainty of not knowing exactly when they might come was so worrisome that I never felt free to relax. Not only was I worried something might happen, but that I might let something slip and tell on them. Internally, I thought that if I made the mistake of telling on them, I would be telling on myself as well.

For many years, I have stressed over having sex with my husband. I think about when it will happen. Until it does, I am so stressed about it. I feel sick. Then, when it happens, I feel happy because it is over. It is so hard to feel good about sex. I wish I could. I want to be happy. I want my husband to be happy. I love him so much. It's hard to explain how I feel. I don't know how to make myself unafraid. I wish I could effectively deal with my conflicted feelings. Whenever I imagine talking with someone about these issues, I get so nervous. I feel like I won't say the right thing and that once people hear what happened, they might say it was my fault. These feelings terrify me.

For years, Katie came to believe that sex would always be related to anxiety, stress, fear and dread. Over time and a tremendous amount of counseling, Katie would begin to feel more normal about her sexuality. A great deal of hard work would be necessary to help her come to terms with normal sexuality, especially since she had taught herself not to feel when engaging in sexual activities. With a great deal of hard work, she would gain a sense of control over her emotions, which had formerly overtaken her with anxiety.

Now, she has a sense of calm that gives her the ability to reach out toward her husband. Challenges are still part of everyday life for Katie. However, she and her husband continue to grow in their intimacy toward one other. She is learning how to reduce her anxiety and is allowing herself to be more relaxed pertaining to physical contact.

If you married an individual who has suffered from sexual trauma, Katie and I would like to recommend the following suggestions relating to sexual activities:

- *Secure counseling services for your mate with a qualified professional. If those services do not include both partners then keep looking until you locate a therapist who deals with the partnership, not just the individual.*
- *Seek physical therapy to help them relax if necessary. Katie enlisted the help of a physical therapist to help reduce painful intercourse.*

- *Remain calm when your mate becomes panicked. Trauma can produce vivid flashbacks that can cause the person to freeze.*
- *Spend time talking with your mate outside the bedroom about what they like or dislike in the bedroom. Never assume you know. Ask.*
- *If at any time during sex your partner "freezes," then stop. Most likely they are having a dissociative experience. Katie describes this as "disappearing" during sex. Katie recommends talking calmly to them so they can "come back" to the room. Kindness and patience are two key ingredients in successful navigation of this difficulty.*
- *Never rush the healing process. Katie has told me that when she felt she could trust her husband to keep her "safe" during sex, she became more comfortable with her self-expression.*

Having a loving, kind, caring, and soft spirit are essentials in helping your mate deal with the past trauma of sexual abuse. These qualities foster hope, growth, and safety needs that fuel healthy relationships. Being aware of your mate's needs will go far in helping them grow toward healing and becoming a more whole person.

Chapter 3

Becoming Fatherless

My mom and dad gave me life. For that I am thankful. However, after arriving on planet Earth it would not be long before my father would rob me of one of life's most precious gifts: my innocence. This theft would start me down a path of not trusting other people. This would create a deficit in my personal development that would damage my mind, personality, and ability to think and speak for myself.

Fathers are supposed to protect, provide, and care for their children. I'm quite sure that I wanted all those things. Who doesn't, right? As hard as I might try, I have never been able to think of one time when I felt safe. How could I? Every day of my life was a waiting game. Who was going to hurt me next? How much was it going to hurt?

Because of my father's poor choices, I was not able to have a life where I felt provided for, cared for, and protected. For whatever reasons, he stood for none of those things to me. My dad became my enemy. There was no one to rely on. Some kids are able turn to their father to help them with their problems. My father was my problem.

If only I had found some way of fighting him. I didn't. The thought of overcoming him was not even possible. He was strong, self-willed, and uncompromising in his pursuit of whatever he wanted. I paid dearly for his lusts. For me, his intentions only represented evil. To this day, he holds no special place in my heart. It hurts my heart to even think about him.

The first time I vividly remember being abused was by my cousins when I was four. However, I later remembered times before when my father touched me. My earliest memories before four years of age were of my father fondling and kissing me. He almost always came in the night. As the door opened, it made a distinctive sound. The first time he opened the door, it didn't scare me because I wasn't expecting anything bad. Every time after that, the sound of the door opening evoked unimaginable panic.

These events always created fear inside of me that would linger. I was just waiting, in despair, for the next time. It is difficult for me to convey how exhausting life was for me. It was like I was living in a war zone with absolutely no protection. I would compare it to being totally exposed, waiting for the death sentence to be executed. The difference between a soldier and myself was that early on in my life I wanted to die so the war would be over. Most soldiers have the will to fight, but any willpower I had was lost in a sea of confusion.

As a young child, around the ages of 8 and 9, I thought about dying every day. Most of my thoughts centered around slitting my wrists, taking pills, or throwing myself in front of a car. Most of these ideas came from watching television. Because I was such a quiet child and unnoticed by adults, I would overhear their conversations. They would discuss what some of the troubled kids at school were doing to harm themselves. These conversations caused me to think specifically about how I might end my life.

As I grew older, ages 12 to 17, I began to think about dying in an accident. Often, I would visualize myself jumping off a building or drowning. When I started to drive, I would imagine myself running off a bridge. Almost every time I was behind the wheel, these intrusive thoughts were filling my mind. Sometimes, the thoughts were fleeting and other times they would last 30 minutes or more. How tiring my life was then.

Think about Katie's youth with me for a moment. She is a frightened, hurting, and unnoticed little girl. She is in the presence of adults who pay little to no attention to her. They discuss issues that a little person should not be overhearing. How many adult conversations occur with children present and with no thought given to how the information will negatively impact the

31

child's mind? Did anyone ever stop to ask why this little girl was so withdrawn? Why didn't she speak? Why was she so unresponsive to people? Did anyone really care?

I want to believe there were kind-hearted people who knew Katie. The problem is they never seemed to show up when Katie needed them. The warning signs were obvious. So, what of the school teachers, school counselors, and other professional people who should have noticed a precious child who could not speak the words that might set her free?

Katie had a very difficult time allowing herself, after so many years of denial, to believe that her dad abused her. It was as if she had walled off that part of her mind, and no one was allowed access, not even Katie. It was not until we utilized Eye Movement Desensitization and Reprocessing (EMDR) that the door to these memories was unlocked.

Let me explain some basic components about EMDR. First, it was Francine Shapiro who developed this therapy. Second, the goal of EMDR is to reduce the long-lasting negative effects of distressing memories by developing more adaptive coping mechanisms. Third, the therapy uses an eight-phase approach that includes having the patient recall distressing images while receiving one of several types of bilateral sensory input, such as side-to-side eye movements, tactile input, or auditory input. Fourth, although EMDR was developed to treat adults with Posttraumatic Stress Disorder, it is also used to treat other conditions and children. Finally, since 2004, EMDR has been *recommended as an effective treatment for trauma in the "Practice Guidelines of the American Psychiatric Association," the Department of Veterans Affairs and Defense, Substance Abuse and Mental Health Services Administration, the International Society for Traumatic Stress Studies, and the World Health Organization.*

EMDR is based on the Adaptive Information Processing model or (AIP). This model stresses that memory networks are the basis of clinical symptoms and mental health. One focus of EMDR is regarding unprocessed memories as the basis of pathology. EMDR is about processing memories. There is a large difference in reliving a memory and recalling one. EMDR seems to assist the client in recalling a memory leading to reprocessing, and thereby reducing the negative effect.

Let me ask that you read the following letter that goes into more detail about her father. The letter reflects on how overwhelming the memories of abuse can be inside the mind of the victim. Her references to the memories she "worked on" is a specific reference to the EMDR sessions.

I wanted to write down what was happening in my head during the last memory I worked on. The memory we started with was my brother taking pictures of me naked when I was about ten. I remember being on my bed without my clothes on in my bedroom. In that house, we had a popcorn ceiling and when I was staring at it I would count the individual pieces. My brother would tell me that he liked the way my body looked. Nothing he said mattered to me at this point. I was beyond caring about anything anyone said about me. Good, bad, or otherwise.

But then, the memory becomes different, but the same. I am on a big bed, but I am really small. It isn't my own bed because it doesn't have the right bedspread, and there is a man in the room. I can see his hands, and I know what is going to happen. I can't see who the man is and I am scared to believe it. It's like everything is dim. That particular experience was like looking into a shadow. My brain did not want to know what was happening or who was doing it. We stopped therapy for the day and you (Dr. Helton) asked me if I knew who was in the memory. I wasn't sure, or I didn't want to know. I think I knew all along that it was my father. But if I admitted that it was him, I would be indicting myself as well. That thought was just too overwhelming to process. It would be too painful.

When I came back to the memory the next day and I tried to focus on it, my mind went to a different memory, which frustrated me. The memory my mind went to was my dad taking me out of the bathtub. I was really scared and threw up on the floor. He spanked me for not making it to the toilet. I remember how angry he became. Maybe his anger that day was because he didn't get his way. I'd like to think so anyway. Even at four, I was anticipating being hurt with no way to fight back.

I remember my mom wasn't home because she was teaching adults who were learning to read. When she came home, I was lying down in my bed. She came to my room and I told her that dad had spanked me because I threw up. She sat down on my bed and stroked my hair. She explained to me that dads didn't know how to handle little girls. Whenever my mom was around, I felt less vulnerable. However, her presence was never enough to calm my fears and quiet my mind from the inevitable.

Did it ever cross my mom's mind to question my dad for spanking a little girl who threw up? What kind of mother would tolerate a father punishing a child for being sick? Instead of taking up for me, my mother's only interest was covering my father's deceitful and cruel actions. My mother must have talked herself into believing that my father's actions were normal. What kind of denial would a person have to be in to not see what was happening to me? Maybe she wasn't strong enough to see what was staring her in the face. She had married a monster.

While in an EMDR session, I went back to the memory of the little girl in the big bed. The little girl was wearing a nightgown. The bedspread had roses on it and I could see and feel the hands touching me. They were my dad's hands. It is still so hard for me to write that. Then, my mind shut down, and I felt like I was spiraling out of control. I was screaming in my head, "Please help me," "Don't touch me," and "I can't do this!" over and over again. My mind was stuck in panic mode. In that moment, I remember hearing Dr. Helton tell me to use my "butterfly taps." The butterfly taps (of EMDR) helped to relieve my anxiety and quiet the screams. As I became calm again, you asked me if it was my dad, and I think I nodded my head up and down. It was extremely hard to acknowledge. I wanted to deny it. I still do.

This memory would be one of our most difficult obstacles to overcome. Katie would have to come to terms with both the betrayal of her father and his lack of protection. Her father had purposefully, willingly, and knowingly chose to sacrifice his daughter's well-being for his own selfish desires. She mentions the "butterfly taps." This is a calming technique used within an EMDR session when a patient becomes flooded with anxiety and is unable to process a specific memory. The client crosses the hands one over the other while interlocking their thumbs. They then place their hands at both clavicle bones and begin to softly tap back and forth. Thankfully, in this instance this technique assisted Katie in returning to a stable emotional state. It provided the means to calm her anxiety and regain her composure while allowing her to continue the difficult work of reprocessing the painful memories. Ultimately, she was able to reprocess each of these difficult memories and can now reflect on them without intense crippling anxiety. Many of our future sessions would focus on her father's molestation and abuse.

When my mom was gone, sometimes at night, my dad would touch me or put his mouth on me. I remember staring at the little lamp in my room until it was over. Although it was dim, it was enough to help take my mind away from what was happening. Sadly, I remember what every light in our house looks like, even to this day. Sometimes I would count until it was over. I didn't understand what was going on. He told me it was our secret.

All children crave the attention of their parents. All I ever wanted was to be loved and protected. Because of my father's abusive actions, I would not understand the concepts of love and protection. Being an object of another's lusts causes a child to believe that they are "bad." Throughout my childhood, I could never pinpoint why I felt "bad," but only that I was "bad." This emotional deceit created an uncommon urge to be someone that was real and not a figment of my imagination.

In a way, I guess I felt special that my father was paying attention to me. Even though it was not what I wanted, it was attention nonetheless. A child that only receives negative attention still craves attention. However, because of his depravity, I was unable to know how to feel normal feelings. There was never a proper example demonstrated to me of how to get the appropriate attention that should exist between a normal father and daughter. Now, I hate him for what he did. But, being so young, I didn't know any better at the time.

When I was about eight, I remember my dad would say something like, "Let's go take the trash to the dump." This was his excuse to get me away from the house. He would always drive the station wagon. After he disposed of the trash, he would take me to a deserted back road. We lived near abandoned bauxite mines, so there were a lot of dirt roads that led to dead ends. He would park behind the hills, put down the station wagon seat and have sex with me. This was the first time I had ever had vaginal sex. It's crazy that I have to qualify that statement. I mean, I had different things like fingers, sticks, toys, screwdrivers, a handle of a hammer, and a curling iron, but that was the first time I had a penis inside of me. It was extremely painful. These trips with my dad happened about five times.

Whenever he would call for me to leave the house with him, I knew where we were going. I felt scared and alone, trapped in a vortex where everything was wrong and there was no way to make it right. It made me feel empty and used and like the world hated me. In my mind, God wanted me to suffer. I always had this feeling that came in the form of a question, "What did I do wrong to make everyone want to hate and punish me?" Somewhere around the age of eight or nine, my dad stopped having sex with me. My theory is that after this time, we started going to church more, and I think my dad was fearful that as we got close to people, someone might find out what he was doing.

The following is a letter that Katie wrote to me after we began the painful work of processing her father's cruelty.

The first days after I had the memory were really hard. I spent some time lying on my closet floor crying. I also felt so tired and mentally drained. I just wanted to sleep. I also felt a little relieved. I didn't have to pretend anymore. I was so overwhelmed with questions and feelings. How could I forget what happened to me? I mean, did I really? Or, did I just hide it from the real me? There are things I know, but don't want to. My dad touched me. He hurt me. When I look at him, I feel sad. I am not ready to forgive him. Can I pretend it didn't happen?

Probably. But I don't want to lie to myself. That's just another way I am chained to the past. Although it hurts and for a while I didn't think I could face life, I know I can. And I don't have to do it alone.

One of the most difficult obstacles for Katie to face came from her father's active abuse. Loss of protection, which should have come from her father, would continually be a challenge in therapy. In our discussions, Katie described the lack of her father's protection as "feeling lost." She never felt "safe" around her father and was scared all of the time. Even when her father was not at home, Katie told me, "There was always my brother to be scared of. He was there all the time." Take a moment and contemplate never being "not scared." The enormity of the fear remains invasive in the mind of the trauma victim. Without help, they often feel crippled as they try to walk through life.

There are no perfect fathers. But there are fathers who care and protect. Katie was never allowed the opportunity to experience the love of a father who only had the best intentions toward his daughter. Her father's presence was a continual reminder of the circumstance of hopelessness and of what would come at his next desire. The loss of protection would damage Katie's psyche deeply. Let me give you an example.

After some time in therapy, as she began to be able to think for herself, she asked me this question: "Do you think I am wrong for feeling like what my Dad did to me was wrong?" When she asked me this question, I was astounded. What! Wrong? How could she be wrong? After thinking about her question, part of the solution to the question occurred to me. After living so many years feeling that she was "in the wrong," she had convinced herself that she was at fault. Others had so imposed their will on her that she was unable to think for herself. When this happens to a person, they begin to feel immense emptiness and sorrow as they grieve the loss of their identity. Identity is the very component of what makes each of us uniquely different from every other person in the world. This was one of the great challenges for Katie—learning to think for herself. Most, I think, take this for granted. Like walking. Most of us just do it. Not so for the wounded warrior who is so injured he or she must learn to walk again. So it was for Katie. The depth of this injury created an upside down world for her in which she would have to learn, for the first time ever, to give herself permission to think for herself.

Once, I asked Katie if she ever stopped and thought, "I made it!" She said, "No. It's kind of like war. You just do what has to be done to get through it." Not every victim "gets through it." Many die in the process of trying to survive the abuse. Others, sadly, take their own lives. Katie lived to share her story in hopes of helping others who have faced the same disturbing circumstances.

I often use the phrase with my clients, "You have to give yourself permission to..." The completion of this sentence is based on whatever their greatest need is at that moment in therapy. For Katie, the sentence was, "You have to give yourself permission to think for yourself again." For her, the idea of allowing herself this fundamental human right had been washed away by the tidal wave of tyranny. For therapeutic purposes, her decision to choose to think for herself would enable us to forge ahead.

Once Katie was able to start this process, new options became available for us in therapy. We could now begin working on boundaries that had been erased and forgotten. For example, prior to this decision, any boundaries related to decisions were always left up to someone else. In other words, Katie's life had been reduced to whatever other people wanted, and she simply followed along. In many sessions, Katie would tell me, "It was just easier to go along with whatever than to fight it." Challenging thoughts like this would become a major focus of treatment. Remember that long held thought patterns, however erroneous, are deeply engrained in the core psyche. A therapist must stay focused on the goal: helping the client toward better mental health. This is a very slow and painstaking process.

One can only imagine how isolated Katie felt, living life as though she would never be capable or allowed to make her own choices. It was agonizing work for Katie to begin to make decisions for herself. We started small and eventually grew toward more difficult decisions, like issues related to her parents and marriage.

People who have experienced such trauma have tremendous

difficulty with making decisions. This complicates their lives, as they are not prone to set good, healthy boundaries for themselves and other people. Subsequently, they may perform self-harming behaviors as Katie did. Or, they may not be sure when to say "yes" or "no" in certain circumstances.

I recall a session when we were working on appropriate boundary setting. She was having a very difficult time with a particular person in her life. She continued to be domineered by this person and would not stand up for herself. In my frustration, I said, "Why don't you fight it?" She responded, "It's just easier to let it happen than to fight it." Hopefully, you can see how skewed one's mind can become when that hopelessness overtakes them.

Unwilling to let this issue go, I pressed forward with resolve, and so did Katie. She mustered the strength to draw a solid boundary of what she would not tolerate. I remember the day she called me to celebrate her victory. "I took up for myself and drew a boundary," she said. "Wonderful," I replied, "How did it go?" Katie's response was, "Not very well. Now _____ is mad at me and pouting." I encouraged her to hold her position and stand her ground. She did. Her friend began to have more respect for Katie, and the pouting stopped. Ultimately, her decision to set a boundary would strengthen their friendship. This decision also helped Katie develop more trust in her ability to decide for herself. It was a win/win situation for her and her friend. This would be the first of many more good decisions to come.

For Katie, making a decision to draw a boundary was one of

the most difficult parts of therapy. She was so unsure of herself. Simply telling a person to have more confidence will not work. I marvel at parents who will tell their child who is scared, "There's no need to be scared." If the child is scared, then they are scared. Why not recognize the fear and proceed to help them overcome it? That is what I chose to do with Katie. I recognized her fear, acknowledged the fear as real, and proceeded from that point to help her overcome. Thanks to Katie's unfailing spirit of resilience, this would be the first of many times she would take up for herself. Thankfully, I have been privileged to witness her growth into greater awareness, and, as a result, a more whole person.

As work continued with Katie, "fear" would be a formidable emotion that would demand our attention. The American psychologist, John B. Watson, investigated "fear" in his famous "Little Albert" experiment. He helped propagate the idea that fear is something we learn. We are not born with it, but we learn it. Admittedly, many of Watson's ideas are controversial. However, if fear is learned, then it's possible to treat fear in a way that lessens its negative impact on any given client. Over time, Katie would learn to "reframe" feelings of fear and dread and begin to take back her life.

Chapter 4

No Way, No Hope

    The first time I had a panic attack, I was eleven years old. I didn't know what a panic attack was then, but I know now. It actually started over something silly. I was fighting with my brother, and we were told to go to our rooms. My brother followed me to my room and slammed my door. He then ran to his room and slammed his door. We both got in trouble for slamming the door. I told my dad that I didn't do it, but he didn't believe me. I freaked out. I think it was because I realized that if he didn't believe me over something that simple, why would he believe me about what was really happening? I started screaming and I couldn't stop. I was rocking back and forth and screaming, and I couldn't control it. I couldn't breathe. I guess I eventually hyperventilated and passed out because I woke up kneeling on my bed. My parents were not concerned with what happened to me. They were just worried that the neighbors might have heard me screaming and thought I was crazy.

Around this time, I made my first friend. She was living in a foster home with a family at church. Her stepdad had abused her, and her mom knew, but didn't stop it. So, she and her siblings were removed from the home. We became very close, and I ended up telling her that my brother had abused me. However, I chose to tell her that it had stopped, and I was fine. I made her promise not to tell anyone, but I secretly hoped she would. She never did. It made me so happy to have a friend. I was relieved. For a short time, having that friend made me feel like the weight of the world was not entirely on me. Someone else could help share the burden of life's struggles.

The following year, she went back to live with her mom. I never saw her again. I remember feeling so sad and lonely when she left. Now, I think that meeting her was when I realized that if I reported the abuse, it could destroy my family. My friend's family had been dismantled. Her stepdad went to prison. She was taken away from her mother. If I told on my family, I might lose them. When you are eleven and twelve years old, the idea of being separated from my family was unnerving and unsettling. If I told on my family, I felt like I would be telling on myself. Everyone would hate me once the news was reported. In my mind, everything that had happened was my fault. Why? Because when you've been told for years that it's your fault, you finally start to believe it.

Did you notice Katie's age when she made her first friend? Eleven. Think about this with me for a moment. What age were you when you made your first friend? I recall being about four or five years of age when I had my first friend. Katie was in the sixth grade. Notice also that her newfound friend would soon be gone. Friendships help us form new attachments and bonds that encourage intellectual and emotional growth. For Katie, her growth in these areas would remain stunted for many years to come. This would have a crippling impact on her emotional well-being.

The fact that Katie had no friends should tell you a great deal about her family system. Katie's family was a one way, closed system. Her father and mother did not allow outside contact with other children her age. This is very typical for families that neglect or abuse their children. There is a fear that they will be "found out." Therefore, the adults maintain the abuse cycle by avoiding contact with people they do not know well.

One of the great challenges in therapy would be Katie's early life decision that it was her fault. She had come to the conclusion that all of this mayhem was because of her existence. Years of being told, "It's your fault" had taken its toll. She was emotionally depleted. Empty. Rebuilding from the foundation up would be a monumental task that would take years.

I also tried to tell my mom that my brother was hurting me. He had kicked me in the crotch so hard it bruised me. She said, "You probably deserved it!" I didn't try to explain it any further.

In my mind, I did deserve it, and she confirmed my suspicions. I decided not to say anything to anyone ever again. Why should I? They wouldn't have believed me anyway. It was easier to just try and bear it than being told you didn't matter.

My relationship with my mother has always been strained. I've always blamed her for not protecting me like she should have. It was damaging to feel like my mom knew what was happening and did nothing to stop it. Now, as a mother myself, I can't grasp how you can knowingly allow your child to suffer. I remember telling my mom that if she died, I wouldn't cry at her funeral. I wasn't trying to be mean. It was just a fact. I felt like I had no connection with her. I couldn't be real with her because there were so many secrets. I still resent her for what she failed to do.

It's hard to explain what living is like on a daily basis when you've been led to believe you really don't matter. People, like a mom and a dad, who are supposed to be supportive, spend their efforts on hurting you. I remember having the feeling at ten years of age that the world didn't need me. The world, meaning my family, didn't care if I even existed. Why should I care? The only place I ever felt safe was when I was away from home at school. Unfortunately, that feeling of security would disappear as well. I recall wanting to die everyday. My particular idea about dying was of jumping off a bridge. This way, maybe no one could find me and I would be lost. I didn't want anyone to find me because then it would be like I never existed in the first place.

Many people wonder why more children don't tell someone of their abuse. Similar to the instance Katie cited above, many of my clients made some effort to let it out, only to be told by adults that it was not true, that they were lying or did not understand. If Katie's mother had investigated further and listened to her, it would have afforded Katie the chance to give more details. Had Katie's words been embraced by her mother, believed and acted on, she would have been spared many more years of suffering. Katie's mother was part of the cover up. Since her mother embraced a lie instead of the truth, the consequences for Katie were catastrophic.

A word to people who care for children, whether it be school teachers, day care workers, school counselors, or even professionals, listen to what the child is telling you. Seldom do young children lie about such things as being molested. Please do not dismiss the child's feelings. There are always reasons behind why a child takes a risk and tells someone about abuse. Care enough to respond. Contact a school official or social worker, or report the information to the department of children's services. At least give the child a chance. More times than not, you will save the child from untold harm.

I found out that my cousins had been caught touching another girl. She went to my cousins' church. I had met her a few times, and my extended family was close to her family. I remember my grandmother had a picture of her hanging on the wall. I can still see her face exactly like it was in that picture. My aunt told my mom that my cousins were caught touching the girl. My aunt just thought they were curious. They promised never to do it again. My cousins thought it was funny that they got away with it. My cousins said that their parents didn't believe the girl, and they would never believe me either. I still feel guilty for not saying anything to help that girl.

I want to share two other instances where I tried to reach out and let someone know what was happening to me. I must admit that I wasn't very keen on revealing family secrets, since no one had believed anything I had said up to this point in my life. When I turned eleven, several events happened in my life that really destroyed what was left of me. It all started with a storm. It was a storm I will never forget, because it seemed to catapult me into an unbearable situation. I remember that day so clearly.

My family went out to eat for breakfast that Saturday. I remember how hard the wind was blowing. When we came out of the store, it was raining, but sunny at the same time.

We went home, and I was watching TV with my mom while eating mint chocolate chip ice cream. My brother was sick with the flu and was in bed. My dad was watching some kind of sports. All of a sudden, my dad came into the living room and said that there was a tornado warning for our county. We didn't hear the sirens, but my dad looked out the back window and said, "There is a tornado in the back yard." We grabbed the couch cushions and all got in the hallway.

I remember my dad going to the back door and locking it, like that was going to save us. It was so loud, the roaring of the wind. The whole house was shaking so hard I could hear the window blinds rattling. Then, it was over. People always say there is silence after a storm. It wasn't. It was raining so hard when my mom opened the front door. I thought the tornado was still occurring, and I made her shut the door. We lived in a wooded area, and all of the trees were flattened. Half of our neighbor's house was gone. Another neighbor's house had been torn in two. There was a trailer park across the main road, and we had heard that there were many injuries. My dad and brother walked over there to help. They were carrying people out using doors as stretchers.

My mom and I stayed behind and covered our roof with the lining of our swimming pool. A tree was lying across the top of our house. Three people died. One was a friend of my brother. The next few weeks were a blur. My parents walked my brother and me out of our neighborhood because there were people looting the houses. We had to be very careful not to step on power lines. We didn't have power or running water for a few weeks. It really scared me, and I was afraid to go outside for a long time.

During this time, my grandparents came to help us clean up. Whenever company came they would stay in my room. I would have to sleep on my brother's floor in a sleeping bag. I always asked to sleep on the couch in the living room, but the grownups wanted to talk and didn't want me in the way. I would try to fall asleep as soon as I could so I wouldn't have to feel my brother touching me. It didn't really work because I knew what was going to happen and was too scared to sleep. At least it protected me from having to participate.

One of the nights, my brother had my pants off. I could feel him rubbing on my bottom. He started to push on me and went inside my butt. It hurt so bad I started screaming. He covered my mouth and kept pushing. It felt like I was being stabbed over and over again. He dragged me to the bathroom with his hand covering my mouth. He kept telling me to be quiet because I was going to wake up my grandparents. I was bleeding into the toilet. He told me to take a bath and left me in the bathroom. Now, I can't believe that he acted like it was my fault. I had a hard time sitting for a week after that happened. My grandparents ended up staying a whole month. My brother forced himself on me every night that month.

The following is a letter of one of Katie's memories when she was twelve years old:

Did you know that I was twelve years old the first time I tried to kill myself? I tried to jump out of my mother's van. I unbuckled my seat belt and opened the door. I would have done it if my mother hadn't grabbed my shirt. Do you think pain is relative? Do you think that people feel pain differently or just that their response is different? Do you think I will be able to totally forgive the people who hurt me? Sometimes I feel like I have, but then all these feelings of anger and hate come up. I wonder if I can truly forgive with malice in my heart. Is it good enough to be trying? Do you ever feel like you are trying so hard to do God's will but keep on failing? Sometimes I still think about giving up.

Her letter to me makes it plain that she continues to struggle with forgiveness. At this point in the process, I tried to assist Katie with processing her feelings. You can tell by reading her thoughts that they are confused and fractured. Allowing her to slowly work through how she felt was a key to eventually dealing with the forgiveness of her perpetrators. Fundamentally, I do not believe it is healthy for a therapist to "rush" a client toward anything that may be a good thing, like forgiveness. Rushing any part of Katie's journey toward healing would ultimately create regression. That is the last thing either of us wanted.

At school, I was having trouble with my attitude. One of my teachers kept me after class for slamming my chair into the table. He was concerned and asked if something was happening at home. I almost told him, but I couldn't. I knew it might ruin my family, so I kept telling myself that I could handle the pain and that I had to be the strong one.

After that summer, I was in the seventh grade. I was asked to join advanced art for the last period of the day. I was in a class of eight. The other students were gifted and on the quiz bowl team, so every Monday, Wednesday, and Friday they would go to quiz bowl while I was alone with my art teacher. My mom actually questioned this predicament and asked me why I was left alone with the teacher. I wonder if my mother was concerned that me being left alone would allow me an opportunity to tell someone about the abuse. I remember telling her not to worry because the rumor circulating at school was that he was gay.

I didn't see anything wrong with being in the class by myself, because it was fun. My art teacher let me play computer games and gave me candy. He started to confide in me about his relationship with his ex-wife and his daughter. He told me about his daughter visiting with him. He also made a point to discuss his girlfriend. The conversation was not really anything out of the ordinary. Receiving attention from anyone at school, even a teacher, was a new and welcomed experience for me. I was desperate to be noticed by someone who just liked me for me. I had no friends at school. No one would talk to me. I walked through each day being so confused about my thoughts and feelings; I'm not sure what kind of person I would have been had someone tried to befriend me. This void inside of me created an insatiable desire for attention.

After a couple of months, he started wanting me to sit on his lap, and he would play with my hair. On days when the other students were present he would talk and laugh with them. On those days, he acted like I didn't exist, like I was nothing. But when we were alone he gave me all his attention. I never made the connection of how manipulative he was, because I did not feel like I had the right to make a choice for myself. In my mind, these things other people wanted me to do had to be done. No matter how depraved it was, "I had to do it."

One day, I was in the art class cleaning paintbrushes in the supply closet. I had the door to the closet open so the light from the classroom lit the closet. The teacher came in and closed the door. Immediately, I knew something wasn't right, because it was totally black in the room. I had paintbrushes in one hand and a jar in the other.

He came up behind me and started fondling me on the outside of my pants. I remember dropping the stuff in my hands and trying to focus on the sound of the water hitting the sink. He pulled down my pants and I completely froze. In my mind I disappeared, as he pushed my body over and raped me. He had his mouth near my ear, and I could hear his breathing and him saying that it felt good.

When he finished, he told me to clean myself up. I had to clean myself with those scratchy paper towels and water. The only light was coming from under the door. Afterwards, I went to my desk and covered my head with my arms.

The next thing I remember was him shaking me to wake up and telling me I was going to be late for the bus.

After that event, it was as if my mind was totally blank. For a long time, I didn't remember what happened. I remembered waking up in the class and that something was wrong, but I couldn't remember anything else. It came back to me in bits and pieces when I was going through therapy years later. He raped me a few more times. He would motion for me to come with him to the back closet. At this point, I just figured that I deserved it because I was a bad person. I remember having the thought that maybe I wasn't a person at all. Maybe I was just an object to be used.

Each day of my life was as if I was dead inside. Feelings were not a part of my life. My life consisted of a list of things that had to be done: Go to school, sit in class, come home, eat, and try to sleep when I wasn't being used and abused, which was also another thing to check off the list. Much of my life was about drifting far away. Being me was too painful. Checking out of my mind and body became the norm.

For me, being hurt by a stranger didn't feel as bad as when my family abused me. That may sound strange to some, but that's how I felt on a daily basis. With family, you have expectations of how they are supposed to be. What the art teacher did to me hurt me and continued to perpetuate the terror I already felt. But, at the same time, it just felt like just another tragedy. I was just one more person for someone else to take his turn and use me. I guess what he did to me was considered rape. At that time, it was just a "whatever" moment. Something I tried to shrug off and forget. Of course, forgetting those events is not something that is easily done.

One time, another boy came with us to an art exhibit at the high school. He helped us set up the exhibit, and we rode in the teacher's truck to get there. I had to sit in the middle and was sitting very close to the teacher. The boy noticed and asked if I thought it was weird that I was the only person in his class. I didn't think it was weird. To me, it was normal. The next week, I was removed from the class and helped with filing in the counselor's office. I still wonder how I was lost and slipped though the cracks. Why did no one question where I was? Why did I always have to be the strong one?

That summer I was at my cousin's house. We were told to play upstairs in his room while the parents talked outside. When my brother, cousin, and I got to his room, he locked the door. He turned his stereo on really loud. He ripped my clothes off me and brought me to the bed. He was rubbing on me and trying to go in me, and I was trying to push him off. My brother came above me and held my hands above me. My cousin pushed himself into me. I remember the song playing on the radio was *The Roof is on Fire.* I looked out the window and could see my parents far below me. I remember wishing they would come save me, but wondering if they would have even helped me if they could.

How could they not know what was happening? Maybe they did know, but it was too hard for them to believe it was true. What about me? Everything in my life was a constant uphill battle to survive and no one seemed to care. Why?

Later that week, my cousins, brother, and I were going exploring. We wanted to find a dam that was down the road. When we were leaving, my aunt called my favorite cousin back. She wasn't allowed to go because we were going to go through the woods and she was allergic to poison ivy. I kept going with them. I guess I didn't think anything was going to happen because we were outside, and they didn't hurt me every time I was with them. I still thought there was a chance things would be normal. We found the dam, but since it was summer, it was mostly dried up with only a little bit of water in the bottom. The walls were made of concrete, and they had to lower me to the bottom of the dam.

We looked around and played in the water a little bit. Then they wanted to do things to me. They took off my clothes. My cousin was rubbing on me and trying to go in me. I was scared, so I kept pushing him away. I told them that I didn't want to do it any more. I was going to tell on them. They got angry and left me there. I tried to get out, but the walls were so high I couldn't lift myself over them. I was scared they were going to leave me there, and the water was going to flood in and kill me.

They had taken my clothes with them, so I was naked. It feels really weird to be naked outside. It made me feel so lonely and vulnerable. After maybe 30 minutes, they came back and said that they would hurt me even more if I did not do what they said. They convinced me that I would be the only one to get in trouble if I told on them. My cousin had me lay down on the concrete, and he had sex with me. I remember how warm and hard the concrete felt under my body. I remember how blue the sky was and how I wished I was flying away.

The last time I remember something happening to me was

when I was 15 years old. I was staying in my favorite cousin's room at my aunt and uncle's house. She was asleep, and I was sleeping next to her. My brother and cousin came into the room and tried to get me to go with them. I refused to go. They put their hand on my mouth and took me with them to my cousin's room. They were angry and said I had to be punished for disobeying. They made me have oral sex with them. They were holding my head and were thrusting their penises down my throat. I kept gagging, and they made me swallow the semen. It made me feel sick. They anally raped me and beat me. When they were done, they pushed me out of the room and threw my clothes out with me. I had blood trickling down my leg and had to go to the downstairs bathroom to clean up. That was the last time I remember any abuse.

We stopped visiting my cousins as much, and my brother started dating, so he left me alone. It did take a while for me to stop being scared. I was still wetting my pants. I slept in my parents' room until I was 14 because I was scared. I never felt truly safe and comfortable in that house, and I still don't. I don't know if I ever will.

The next time in my life that I thought I might be able to share what was happening to me came when I was sixteen years old. My mother made the decision to take me to a counselor because I was scared of storms. Frankly, I was scared of lots of things that I kept inside. All my life I never felt as though anyone really cared for me, including my mom. Both my parents traveled with me to see the counselor.

Now, you will read from one of Katie's journals, which gives you insight into the inner workings of her mind.

I feel overwhelming anxiety in everything I do. I don't go one day in my life without thinking about what happened. Sometimes I hate myself so much. I feel so screwed up. I hate having sex, and I know it kills my husband. I can't help it. Even if I enjoy it, I always end up feeling disgusted with myself after it happens.

To survive my abuse, I locked my feelings away. I have a hard time blaming my brother for what happened. He was just a kid, too. Sometimes I am mad at him. It makes me very angry that it ever happened in the first place. After it stopped happening, I thought I could forget. Every time I had a thought I would tell myself that it didn't happen and to forget it. I didn't want to be one of those people who let it affect their lives. I space out a lot. Most of the time, it is done unconsciously. I will just kind of wake up in the middle of a conversation and not know what the other person is saying. I feel so stupid for not telling. It lasted so long. I was so old. Why didn't I get help?

I feel like I should be punished over and over again for being bad. Maybe I deserved it. These thoughts were being rehearsed in my mind on a daily basis. What made them do that? How did they know about that sexual stuff so early?

After arriving at the counselor's office, we were seated in the waiting room. My parents must have thought I was doing poorly because they didn't believe in counseling and were embarrassed to be there. Neither of my parents was asked to come into the counselor's office. Once I was called back, the counselor discussed with me my fear of storms. He kept saying, "What we talk about in here is private, and you shouldn't talk about it either." He let me leave and brought my parents in only to tell them everything I had just said. I never saw the logic in that.

My parents took me for a second visit. The counselor told me he would try to help me learn how to breathe right. He insisted that I wasn't doing it right. He had me lay on the floor and lifted up my shirt and began to touch my breasts. I got really scared and had a million thoughts rush into my mind all at once. I was frozen. When he tried to undo my pants I hurried back to the couch. I distinctly remember him saying, "You know you can't tell anyone what happens in here." Of course, I never did tell anyone until I told Dr. Helton.

After getting in the car I told my parents I would kill myself if I ever had to go back. Thankfully, my parents never made me go back to that counselor.

What you have just read is an overview of Katie's life, not an exhaustive account of the brutality she suffered at the hands of her biological family and by those in the helping profession. I can promise you that revealing more details only paints a more gruesome picture of the depth of her suffering. This is part of the reason why successful therapy was so difficult. At each turn of her narrative the weight of the trauma blurred her clarity for hope.

Often Katie would ask me if I ever thought she was going to get better. "Absolutely," I would reply. The journey toward well-being for any client is a process, not an event. Resolution does not come all of a sudden. It comes through painstaking work, day by day, toward a better version of oneself. One of the greatest challenges would be helping Katie to begin to think differently about her individual personality and how to move forward in a transformative way.

Chapter 5

Escape To Fantasyland

I decided to go to college out of state because I wanted to get away from my family. One of the main reasons for getting away from my family was that I wanted to reinvent myself. Growing up, I was always shy and reserved. It was scary to even speak to people because of my fear. Would I say the wrong thing? That constantly plagued me.

After arriving at college it was like stepping out of darkness into a really bright light. Up until that time, I never saw myself getting a chance to be in a different situation. Life at home was depressing and hopeless. At college, I made a decision to push away all the bad feelings related to my family, situation, and personality and become a completely different person. This was not a snap decision. For quite some time before going to college,

I would dream about making a change in the way I lived life. I called it hopeful expectations.

College life was a new beginning for me. I learned to do things I never even dreamed would be possible. I joined a social club and played intramural sports. On one team I was even elected as the captain for my club. When I met my future husband, he said that he saw me as the "leader" of my group of friends. Although I had never even been allowed to have opinions before, now I not only had opinions, but people seemed to like me. Having to deal with these newfound feelings was very strange.

This atmosphere was a new start for me. I was on the path of becoming everything I always wanted to be. Carefree and fun are two words that come to mind when I recall my entrance into this strange new world. All of a sudden, making friends became easy. Being the life of the party was now a norm for me. For the first time in my life, I discovered a part of me that was exciting and alive. Looking back, it's hard for me to believe how different I was in college compared to what I was before I left home. It was like I was a shell of a person before my collegiate experience. Prior to leaving home, I had never felt like a real person. Life for me was one day after another of hopelessness. It never occurred to me that I could choose to be anything other than scared all the time.

Before going to college Katie was in a lose/lose situation. No matter what she did or how hard she tried to make a situation or relationship better, it was bound to fail. Once she found herself in a new and even exciting situation in college, those days of unwanted bondage seemed to be over. For the first time in her life, her captors were not present, and she could make decisions on her own. This was to be the most exciting period in her life. Her freedom, unfortunately, was to be short-lived.

Around my new friends, I felt a feeling of security. They wanted me to be happy and fun-loving. So, I made the decision to be what they wanted me to be. Anytime I was separated from them and by myself, I felt overwhelmed with everything. It felt as though I was juggling two different lives, which I was. The dilemma was dealing with who I wanted to be and the reality of who I truly was. I learned to be a major pretender. This must have been some way I was trying to cope.

Coping is the key to understanding how Katie was able to alter her personality. It was a way to deal with a new situation and to resist thinking about the old situation. One can simply fill the time with endless activities and people who don't know what's happened to you and have fun. Hiding the facts about her past was easy because no one knew her. This new world provided numerous opportunities for Katie.

I began to feel that safety and security were becoming a part of my new life. I had never felt safe before. While I was growing up, I was never allowed to lock my door. I never felt as though I had any right to privacy. At college, I was able to lock a door and feel a sense of security. It's very hard to describe how good that felt. The feeling was like, "Nobody can get me now." This sense of security allowed me to get restful sleep. Peaceful sleep was not an experience I ever had as a child. When you live in constant fear, sleep is never your friend. It is difficult for me to recall ever being able to sleep soundly the whole night when I was a child. This new atmosphere calmed those fears, and good sleep was something I began to enjoy.

To an unsuspecting person it may have appeared that Katie was carefree, which was far from the truth. She was simply pretending. Admittedly, she may have found a false sense of security while pretending, but no inner healing had taken place. The scars of sexual trauma had cut her heart and damaged her self-esteem and self-image so badly that it was becoming difficult for her to keep hiding the family secrets.

Now, some might ask the question, "How could I prove the validity of my insights?" Good question. The answer lies in adding up the details. Once compiled, the specifics of her case clearly point to severe sexual abuse. As you continue to read, the narrative will continue to shape the overall picture leading one to conclude traumatic abuse.

After dating my future husband for about a month, I made the decision to tell him what had happened in my life. My concern was for him to have a chance to go ahead and get out of the relationship before things got complicated. It was becoming obvious that he wanted to get more serious with me. Once again, the thought of sharing family secrets terrified me. Making the words come out of my mouth was something I didn't know I could do.

One evening we went for a walk. I wanted to tell him in the darkness because I wanted my face to be hidden as much as possible. It seemed easier if he couldn't see me. Then I said, "I have something to tell you. My brother sexually abused me." That was the first time I remember hearing those words come out of my mouth. He responded by expressing his sorrow for me. His response relieved me. At that point, I felt I could begin to trust him because he believed me. Ten months after that walk, we would marry.

Think about the immense risk Katie took by telling her boyfriend about what had happened to her. Once, I asked her what made her tell him about what had happened. Her answer: "I wanted to be honest with him." I've always admired that courageous side of Katie. She risked everything to be honest. Her boyfriend could have very easily said, "I'm sorry that happened, but I didn't sign up for this," and left her. Katie was well aware that she was taking a risk that could end the relationship. She chose to move ahead with sincere honesty. That decision would be very useful in her marriage, as there would be plenty of fallout between her and her husband, due to her abusive past.

One suggestion I give any couple, when one has been abused, is to seek good counseling before entering marriage. Katie and her husband's new marriage would mark the beginning of some very turbulent times. It would have been much better had they obtained skills that would have made the transition to marriage much easier. Since they did not choose to do premarital counseling, the new relationship began without the added value of professional help. One can easily see why so many of these marriages do not survive. Fortunately, Katie and her husband are still married and continue to grow.

Both Katie and her husband did make an attempt at post marital counseling. More details will be provided later. I might add that just because a couple secures pre-marital counseling does not ensure a successful marriage. This is especially true if one or both spouses have had traumatic sexual abuse. Oftentimes clergy/ministers who mean well are ill-equipped to diagnosis and treat complex trauma issues. When considering a counselor for any type of therapy, one must thoroughly research their skill sets before deciding how best to proceed.

On a special note: I have had clients come to me stating that their previous counselor had used EMDR to treat them. When asking the client for clarification, it was evident that their previous counselor was not following proper protocol for proper EMDR treatment. A word of caution: ask to see a clinician's credentials. Those who are actually practicing the proper protocols will be more than happy to have a client review their credentials.

Any counselor who is hesitant or unwilling to allow a client to view credentials should be avoided and if necessary, reported to the mental health board. If a counselor publicizes that they offer specific services, they should produce the proper paperwork for the clients they are serving.

Chapter 6

Dying to Live

Many people who find themselves in perpetual pain seek ways to cope and alleviate the pain and suffering. Oftentimes, these people resort to what we call "self-harming behaviors." These behaviors come in many different shapes and sizes. Clients have been known to inflict pain and cut various parts of their bodies with sharp objects. Many will use a razor of some type. Why would someone intentionally inflict pain on herself? Good question. Some think that since the emotional pain is so great, the abused person should not want any more additional pain. Keep in mind that Katie, and others like her, is not dealing with common pain, so the response is often uncommon. By common pain I mean the normal hurts we all have as a result of normal relationships (e.g. breakups, disagreements, etc.). Uncommon pain is the result of abuse. Below you can read Katie's response *on "cutting."*

I started hurting myself at an early age. At age nine, I would pinch myself because it required no tools. I would use pinching as a method to cope while my abusers were taking advantage of me. In some way it made me feel better. I just wanted to be in control of something. Pinching was a way to focus on what I was doing and not on what they were doing. It was like I was substituting one pain for a different kind of pain. The difference was that, when I was pinching, I was in control.

Cutting is a hard topic to write about. It is embarrassing to me. It's something some people don't understand. There were times that I would cut, usually with a razor blade or box cutter, to remind myself that I was alive. Sometimes I cut to stifle the pain inside my head. The pain from a cut would make me forget about the painful memories, even if it was only for a second. I craved that second of painful bliss.

Another way I would try to control things was by not eating. When I withheld food from myself, it felt like I was in control of something. My life always seemed to be spinning out of control.

Without guidance, many people who are experiencing devastating trauma will resort to these tactics, which never deliver the intended result: permanent relief of suffering. If you can try and understand the need for control, you can better understand why a person would hurt himself or herself like this.

Control is central to understanding self-harming behaviors.

Frequently, a person who has been severely abused has little to no healthy coping skills that allow them to navigate their emotional swings. They become desperate to have a sense of control. When daily living puts them in a constant state of flux, their desperation takes on a life of its own. Sadly, it often becomes deadly. The challenge for the therapist will be to assist in processing those emotions and helping the client to learn new coping skills. This process is extremely slow but critical to the client's overall success. Patience on the therapist's part is crucial to the progress of the client.

Read the following letter Katie wrote to me as she would journal between therapy sessions. Notice the abusive elements and also her longing toward greater mental health and stability.

I want to write down what I now remember. I don't know why, but it just makes me feel better. It's like a way to organize my thoughts. My mom would volunteer in the evenings, and my dad would be in charge of putting my brother and me to bed. He would let us sleep in my parents' bed because there was a TV in their room.

He started by just touching me while he would lie next to me. Then, he started putting his mouth on me. At first, the things he did didn't hurt. Then, he started having sex with me. Sometimes my brother would be asleep next to me when he did it. Other times I would be in my own bed. Sometimes he would want me to sit on his lap. As I think about it now, I want to die. He was always nice and didn't want to hurt me.

We moved when I was seven. My mom was less involved with the community, but my dad continued the abuse. I guess I was eight. He did weird stuff when I was a teenager. We weren't allowed to lock our doors to the bedroom or bathroom. He would knock, but then just come in when I was changing or in the shower. Then, he would just stay there and finish talking to me instead of apologizing and leaving like a normal person. He would also say weird things, like telling me it was normal if I wanted to sleep naked.

Am I just unlovable? Nobody thought I was worth the care and respect to refrain from hurting me. Do you know how much it hurts to realize that people treated you worse than one would an animal? Sometimes I feel like I am nothing, like it is easier to feel like I am not real than to be a person who couldn't be loved. I am scared that it will always feel like I am being stabbed in the chest when I think about the things that happened to me. I want the nightmares to stop. I am tired of waking up crying or confused. I am tired of only getting a few hours of sleep because I am scared of what my dreams will unravel. I am mad at myself for not remembering. Sometimes I am scared that there is more stuff stuck in my head. Having all these feelings at once makes me feel out of control.

Don't worry. I know that I am not a bad person, and I know I will get through this. I think I just need some help. I need to know that it will get better, that I won't hurt like this forever. I know you've said it a million times. I might need you to say it a million more because right now you are one of the few people I trust even more than myself. I need help.

I am not sure how long it took Katie to trust me, but it was months. This letter begins to show traces of hope for the future. For so many months, Katie struggled to believe she would ever recover and feel normal. This is where the persistence of the therapist can make all the difference in a positive outcome. Katie needed to hear that life was going to get better, even if she didn't believe it at that moment. At this point in therapy, the cutting behaviors were beginning to diminish. Her healthy eating habits slowly returned to normal. Painstakingly, Katie was reclaiming her "lost life."

Chapter 7

Wrestling With The Almighty

Meanwhile, I was still struggling with the concept of forgiveness. Throughout my childhood and adult years, I had always strived to do God's will. I didn't understand why God didn't stop the bad things that happened to me. I didn't blame God. I just didn't fully trust God. I always thought I wasn't good enough to be a part of God.

God has always been a part of my life, but He felt like an abstract figure. I believed in him, but I wasn't exactly sure what His role was in my life. When I was a child, I wanted to trust God, but I couldn't. I remember thinking that God didn't care about me. He couldn't.

Early on in my life, I prayed that God would make the pain stop. When I was pretty sure that wasn't going to happen, I prayed that God would just let me die. I figured He couldn't stop the pain, but if I was dead I couldn't feel it either. My life was spent asking, "Why?"

The only answer I could come up with was that God didn't care. When I got older and studied the Bible more, I began to understand the concept of free will. I thought that maybe what I had been through wasn't because of God. Maybe it was from Satan and man's evil desire. I didn't understand how God could love a person like me. I didn't understand that I could do nothing and God would love me. I'm just now beginning to see God's endless love for me. Embracing these thoughts brings me peace.

Below is a letter that Katie sent to me regarding some of her spiritual feelings.

I started reading the Bible, and I realized some things. I grew up reading and studying the Bible. In all actuality, I was reading the words but not hearing what God was saying. I allowed other people to tell me what God is about without really trying to know Him for myself. I always assumed God was scary and someone I would never know. He didn't really care, especially about me. I guess it is easy to categorize God with your feelings about man. My mind limits God with what I *feel* is true, but not the truth. So, I am interested in the real God, not the God in my head, but the God of the Bible. I also have decided that there is no reason to think that I am a horrible person. This doesn't mean I am on the "Katie is awesome" band wagon, but maybe I can make it there one day. I had decided that because bad things happened to me

I was a bad person, undeserving of love, especially my own. I always felt like I could have done more to stop what happened, but the truth is if I could have done more to keep it from happening, I would have done it. I was trapped against my will. It wasn't my fault, and it wasn't God's fault. It almost hurts to admit that I was innocent, as silly as that sounds. Maybe it is hard to realize that I have limited myself for no reason. Maybe if I allowed myself to trust in God, I wouldn't be so selfish.

Am I allowed to love myself? I know I keep asking, but it is such a foreign concept. It's like telling my kids it is all right to do something they have never done before. They are unsure and a little scared, even though I know they will love it. So, is it possible that most of the answers to my struggles can be found in the Bible? That maybe if I focus on fixing my spiritual life everything else will fall into place? Don't worry. I am not delusional. My problems are not over, but it does give me hope.

As you read this letter, hopefully you will notice that struggle, insight, and hope are all mixed together. At this point in therapy she is beginning to become aware of many new feelings and insights that were not previously accessible due to her abuse. For so many years, she was never allowed to have an opinion of her own. She would be told to "be quiet," "don't tell anyone," "we'll get into trouble if you tell," to name a few. For Katie to begin to feel was and sometimes still is, in her words, "scary." It's as if she is waking up in a foreign land where she doesn't speak the language and has to start over learning how to speak. These

insights will continue to emerge from her heart as she continues
treatment.

For those who believe in God and have suffered trauma, it is
very natural to ask questions of God. Katie would ask me
questions like, "Why didn't God stop them? Where was God
when I needed Him? How could God let this happen to me? Did
I do something wrong to make this happen to me?" On and on
the litany of questions would emerge. Slowly, we would work
through her questions. Sometimes she would be completely
satisfied with my explanations. Other times we were both left
wondering. A word here for people who are trying to help trauma
victims: It's all right if you cannot answer every question to your
clients' or friends' satisfaction. Often I would admit to Katie that I
was not sure or simply just did not know how to answer one of
her questions. Sometimes just being there to walk with them in
that place of insecurity is enough. When they know that you care
enough to be there for them, it can work wonders.

Let me share with you another letter concerning God and her
feelings:

I am so angry with everyone, and I don't know why. I want to
feel love toward people, but I can't. This, in turn, makes me mad
at myself for being mad for no reason. I am mostly mad at God. I
have all these scary thoughts in my head that are messing with all
my ideas of right. It's hard for me to see that God cares about us
at all. I wonder if He has just given up on us. And He cared for
us so much that He sacrificed His son for our sins. But to be

honest, that doesn't seem like that big of a deal sometimes. At least He had an intention for the greater good in mind when His son died. People are watching their children suffer and die every single day. And they don't get to have their children back in three days. Is there something wrong with me that I think like this? Is it wrong that I question God's motives, God's plan? I am even embarrassed to write these thoughts down, but I want to try to think past these things. Reading the Bible makes me somewhat angrier. It seems like women are often treated like crap. Oh yeah, you can have a thousand wives, thumbs up to you, but a woman gets caught in adultery, and it's a crime punishable by death. No wonder women are raped. We are just property anyway, right? We get traded like goats or war spoil. I am trying to see the good and pure and righteous God. I want to believe because it is the Truth instead of believing "just in case." It's hard to believe that God is interested when I keep dreaming of people hurting me. Do you know what it is like to wake up and not know where you are or who you are? And to always be scared, terrified of going to sleep. To know that no matter how in control of your life you are when you are awake, that you still have no control of your dreams when you sleep. To realize that you don't really have many dreams anymore, you just have memories. I wake up in the morning exhausted mentally, emotionally, and spiritually because of the terror of the night before. When I see my kids in the morning, I am already reaching into my reservoirs of "pretending to be okay," just so I don't explode. It makes it easy to see how maybe Hell would be better than this. I'm sorry.

I know it isn't right to think this way. I just don't want to do this anymore. I am not even sure if I am tired of living or tired of wanting to die.

Receiving these types of letters is unsettling for a therapist. What you've just read is very similar to what I would hear in many of our sessions together. Often our sessions would be filled with the language of gloom, despair, hopelessness, struggle to live, apparent inconsistencies in people, and so on. When Katie started to uncover much of her buried past, the sessions became a tug of war between what she thought might be right and what she knew to be right. Frequently, she would vacillate between feeling convinced of a thought and then quickly giving up on the thought and returning to uncertainty. As her therapist, helping her navigate the difference between fact and fiction was a fine line.

Chapter 8

Trying, Tiring and Turbulent Therapy

I had decided that I would never tell anybody what happened to me because it would cause more hurt to my family, and I felt like I could handle it. It was my burden to bear. I decided that I would forget about it. Pretend it didn't happen. I convinced myself that it wasn't that bad and didn't hurt that much. If I couldn't keep it to myself, I was weak.

However, during my teenage years I found my best friend. We were so much alike. We were socially awkward and quiet, and we really understood each other. I was 15 when I told her what happened to me. I was very vague and didn't tell her who had been hurting me. I could tell she didn't know what to say, so she really didn't say anything. I didn't mind. I knew it was a hard thing to know and talk about. Later, when we were older, she apologized and told me she was there for me if I ever needed to talk. I also feel like she helped me survive my teenage years. There were many times when I thought of suicide, but I didn't want to leave my friend behind. She is still my friend today.

I was still able to block out some of what happened by forcing the thoughts from my mind when they came in. Then I went to college. It was the first time in years I felt safe. I was free to pretend to be anyone I wanted. I made friends and was mostly happy because I had part of me hidden from everyone, even myself. I became very close to one of my friends and was able to write down some of what happened. She wanted me to seek help from a therapist, but I refused because of what the other therapist had done to me. I felt that she also became weirdly involved with my story. She constantly wanted me to tell more about what happened, even though I was really uncomfortable. I learned that some people like to kind of feed off of your own pain, and it can become obsessive.

I was also afraid to tell a therapist for fear that they would tell me it was my fault. I had already engrained the idea that it was my fault. Actually, I didn't really even think that I was abused. In my mind, it was just something that happened to me because I was a bad person. In my way of thinking about it, abuse happened to people who didn't deserve it. This twisted way of perceiving life is the result of sexual trauma. So, since I believed I deserved what had happened to me, it made sense that I was the one in the wrong, not my perpetrators.

The first time I went to therapy by my own choice was in college. My fiancé and a friend had strongly encouraged me to get help. I went to a female therapist because I thought I would be more comfortable working with another female. My fiancée came with me because I was nervous. The therapist was agitated that I didn't come alone. She said, "Well, if you are really serious about therapy, you would have come by yourself." She seemed to think I was using my fiancé as a crutch, which I guess was true. To be perfectly honest, I was simply terrified of telling anyone the family secrets. The therapist also told me that she preferred teaching in the classroom instead of counseling and the only reason she counseled was because that was part of her university contract.

Let me make some brief comments about therapists and treatment.

First, for a counselor to say, "Well, if you are really serious about therapy, you would have come by yourself," is an absurdity. For a counselor to tell a client they prefer teaching and only counsel because they are being "made to" by the university violates ethical standards and best practices. Certainly, the brash comments of the counselor were discouraging to Katie and hindered the therapeutic relationship before it even began.

Second, think about Katie's mental state. She's terrified of talking to someone she doesn't know. She feels like a counselor will turn anything she says around and that the abuse will somehow be her fault.

Third, it should be glaringly obvious why she wanted her fiancé to come with her for emotional support. However, the counselor, for whatever uneducated reason, concluded Katie was not serious about counseling. Clearly, this counselor had little to no training in effective intake measures before making such a pathetic conclusion. Is it any wonder why so many people, like Katie, become increasingly frustrated with counselors?

As in any profession, there are highly trained and effective counselors, as well as poorly trained and ineffective ones. Katie and her fiancé struggled with a limited selection of counselors, due to little to no ability to pay for services. Therefore, she sought out the services of a counselor who had been hired by her university. Although Katie's parents had insurance for counseling services, she was afraid to tell them. She feared they would think she had failed at life and that they would find out that she was telling the "family secrets."

Oftentimes, I will treat clients on a pro bono basis. My philosophy has always been that I will not refuse treatment simply because of a client's inability to pay. So, let me encourage you to seek out the most highly trained and effective counselors and ask if they would be willing to accept a sliding scale fee or, if necessary, pro bono work. It never hurts to ask for financial considerations. There are many therapists that are driven by compassion and a true desire to help others even when those individuals cannot compensate the provider. Rule of thumb: Ask a practitioner about payment before entering a counseling relationship.

The counselor asked me why I had come, and I shut down immediately. Words would not come out of my mouth. My fiancé took me aside and reminded me why we had come. When it came down to it, my fiancé had to explain the details because I couldn't speak the words. I nodded a lot. It felt like I was "floating" and not completely present in the moment. Fear overwhelmed me as I sat there. My greatest fear was that the counselor would blame me for what happened. After hearing the details, her response was that since the boys were close to my age, it probably was mutual consent. Her words ripped my heart open. The pain was unbearable. Crushing. My fiancé, who eventually became my husband, got extremely angry and told the counselor that she was wrong. Before we left, she said that if I was serious about getting help, I was to come to the second session alone.

Surprisingly, I did make a second visit. My main reason for returning was because of the insistence of my fiancé. Upon my arrival, the counselor said she didn't expect me to come back. She said there wasn't any way we could work on my childhood memories because of the intensity of my anxiety. She suggested that we start by dealing with the anxiety, and that's what we did. I met with her every week for an entire semester.

At one of our sessions, I recall her saying she didn't expect me to come back and that she could no longer help me. She seemed annoyed that I came back. The result of meeting with this therapist was everything I had always dreaded. To share my most excruciating pains and not be believed was almost as devastating as the actual abuse. At that moment, there was a tremendous feeling of defeat that set in on me. What I had hoped would bring relief actually brought about the reverse: pain. In my mind, I was done with going to therapists. I hated them.

Sadly, this counselor set a negative tone from the very first session. Telling Katie that she did not want to counsel students charted the course toward negative outcomes. This is precisely what happened. The fragile therapeutic relationship quickly deteriorated. This counselor should have been removed from her position. Often these types of ethical violations go unreported. It took all the courage Katie could summon just to attend the first session. It's easy to understand why Katie would not want to report this counselor. In fact, until therapy with me, she did not even know that reporting a counselor for wrongdoing was an option.

At the urging of my fiancé, I met with another therapist throughout the summer. Because of my previous experiences, I was reluctant to meet with any therapist. Honestly, I was afraid my fiancé would break up with me if I didn't go. I was totally messed up and was not in denial about that. It seemed to make sense at some level that I should try to get help with my issues before I married.

The counselor asked me to write down things that I remembered because I was starting to recall more events from my past. She gave me a workbook and I would answer the questions. She would read what I wrote and talk to me about it. Most of the time I just sat there and listened without responding. One aspect about her that I appreciated was that she said she believed me. As much as I wanted to be believed, I left that experience still a skeptic. I still was unsure if she was being honest in her response toward me.

My next experience with therapy was not until the third year of my marriage. My husband and I were having difficulty in our marriage, and we made the decision to get marriage counseling. At this time, we were fighting about me cutting myself. He took everything that was wrong with me and made it about him. In other words, he blamed himself for all the things that were wrong with me. As you can imagine, I blamed myself for what he was feeling. This was an unhealthy pattern I developed as a child. Adults were constantly blaming me for any and everything that was connected to sexuality. Needless to say, I was in a very dark place and could not see my way out. My feelings were as if I were a prisoner in my own mind with no means of ever getting out and being free from these tormenting cyclical beliefs.

Much of our difficulties revolved around sex. For me, having sex involved intense fear, crying, physical pain, and flashbacks of my abuse. At this point in my life, I simply believed it was "my duty" to have sex, no matter how it made me feel. The sexual abuse had skewed my thinking. My perpetrators constantly told me, "You have to have sex with me." That type message was a consistent force in molding my views about my role during sex and the unhealthy views toward sexuality.

For me, sex was just something "I had to do." The abuse had stolen my voice, and in my mind I had no say about anything regarding sex. This also extended into intimacy issues. Any time my husband would touch me, I would recoil, get up and leave, or at times just freeze. As you can imagine, this did little to promote relational well-being in our marriage. Neither he nor I had any idea of how to work together to improve our desperate situation. Once again, we found ourselves reluctantly seeking help by trying to find another counselor.

The choice of a counselor was made based on who was on our insurance and who could meet after work. This is not the best approach in making a selection of a counselor. At the time, though, it seemed to be our only option. Now, I would advise people to do some homework, ask your medical doctor's advice or talk to a trusted friend who has had a good experience with a counselor. Any of these decisions have a certain amount of risk. However, the risks outweigh simply choosing blindly from a long list of names.

We chose a male therapist due to our last negative encounters with the female therapist who wanted to be a teacher and not a counselor. After my husband and I had a few sessions with the new counselor, the determination was made that most of our problems were related to my abuse. At the suggestion of the therapist, I met with him for about one year. I never told the therapist or my husband that I was terrified to meet alone with a male therapist. I had made the decision that I wanted to become a healthier individual, no matter how terrified I felt. I wish the therapist had taken Dr. Helton's approach and offered to allow another supportive person to sit in on the session. This would have helped allay my fears considerably.

During our sessions, I wrote down more of what happened to me, but I was hardly ever able to discuss any of my feelings with the therapist. It was my impression that he really didn't know what to do to help me. During the sessions, he never took any clinical notes, which I often wondered why. At the beginning of every new session, he seemed to want me to review our previous session, as if he didn't remember what we had covered. I really think if he had taken notes, it would have enhanced our time and effort tremendously.

Once, he told me that it was fine for my husband to view pornography by himself and if I agreed, it was okay for him to do so. Because the counselor was supposed to be a Christian and said it was okay, I took his word as truth. Since I didn't want to have sex, I was fine with my husband engaging in pornography. Although I wasn't sure if that was the right attitude, I desperately needed some relief from how traumatizing sex made me feel. If I knew my husband was masturbating to pornography, maybe it would take pressure off me. If he was being pleasured by another outlet, I might not have to have as much sex with him.

Let me tell you from first-hand experience that if your

husband is doing this, you should confront him, deal with it, and get professional help rather than push the issue away. Once you tell your husband its okay, it's very hard to say, "I have changed my mind and want to take it back." As you might imagine, this series of developments did little to improve the overall good health of our marriage.

This is a case of unethical behavior on the part of the counselor. The suggestion of pornography being acceptable only made their marriage worse. It alienated the couple from one another. The counselor's opinion became "law" for the husband to trade intimacy with his wife for pornography. Clearly, the therapist was not well-versed in how to enhance couple's closeness, and he created the exact opposite. Any therapist should tread very carefully when discussing matters of couple intimacy. Providing suggestive implants should be avoided. The therapist should be acting as a "guide on the side" and not the "sage on the stage." Clearly, this mental health professional overstepped the boundaries on ethical behavior and suggested ideas that harmed the clients. A better approach would be to assist the client in exploring options, ultimately allowing them to make their own choice.

One helpful suggestion the counselor gave was that I might try physical therapy to deal with the extreme pain during intercourse. Because I was embarrassed to face my regular gynecologist, I made an appointment to get a referral with a brand new doctor. I just couldn't bear the thought of explaining what I needed to do. So, going to a complete stranger seemed to be a better choice. She referred me to a specialist who had experience with trauma cases.

My counselor had written a note for me to take to my doctor visit. The note said that I had been sexually abused and couldn't talk with anyone about it. Once the specialist read the note, she knew what I needed. I clearly remember being on the examination table and being completely gripped by fear. I recall being so embarrassed that I was even in this situation. The exam was extremely painful. Thankfully, my husband was present and that helped to calm me somewhat.

After being examined, I was referred to a physical therapist. Thankfully, the therapist was a female. The doctor that examined me explained my situation to the physical therapist. At the time, I could not even say the words "sexually abused." So, the doctor helped me transition to therapy by informing the therapist of the details.

Before my first visit, I was so scared I was physically shaking. I entered the clinic so scared and could not stop myself from trembling. The therapist specialized in helping sexually abused patients. I remember her telling me that she dealt with this all the time. Because I was so nervous, her words did little to relieve my anxiety. One of the things she did that really helped me was explain each and every aspect of the therapy she was going to perform prior to proceeding. This gave me a sense of what was going to happen without having to guess. She was very kind.

The physical therapy did help me learn to relax my body during sex. Intercourse went from being very painful to being endurable, without immense pain. I still did not enjoy sex. Other than recommending physical therapy, the counselor offered no ideas of what could help me cope in my marriage or my personal life. The lack of help tired me, and I eventually quit therapy. At this point, I came to believe that therapy could help other people, but not me.

When should a counselor refer a client to another specialist? When no progress is being made and/or the couple is getting worse. Katie would tell me that this therapist never asked her to set goals or anything resembling structure. Lack of direction and clear goal-setting should assist clients in being able to measure progress. Again, the therapist failed Katie in a most unprofessional way.

After six years of marriage, I was constantly having panic attacks. Super depressed. I wanted to be a hermit and live underground. Thinking about leaving the house would cause debilitating anxiety and depression. Thinking about talking on the phone would make me so scared. I don't know why. I didn't have any friends. In my most disparaging times, I wanted to die, but I was afraid I would go to hell. There were other times when life seemed hopeless, and I would try to think about my kids to combat my desire to die. Feeling so hopeless, it was becoming easier to convince myself that I deserved to go to hell.

At this point in my life, I was barely functioning. I had two children, ages 1 and 3. Leaving the house consisted of going to the grocery store and church. This was only because I felt as though I had to. My life consisted of going back and forth between the bed and the couch. While on the couch, my child would bring food to me that he wanted, and I would open it so he could eat. Every day, without exception, I wanted to die. My fear about killing myself was that my children would blame themselves for my death. I was convinced that being a "sorry" mom to them was better than being no mom at all. If I hadn't had kids, I would have already given up long before this point. Dying seemed so much easier than living.

Living daily life for me was pure torture. No social life. No support. Even when I went to church, I talked to no one. Most people probably thought I was stuck up. Those people could not even begin to realize how scary living life was for me. Imagine living your whole life not trusting anyone, never knowing if someone might hurt you. In my mind, being close to people would only mean it was a matter of time until I would be hurt or used again.

Someone once asked me why Katie was getting worse when the physical abuse from her family was no longer happening. It is important to note that although the physical abuse from her family had stopped, Katie was becoming increasingly more mentally unstable. The abuse acts like a cancer. Although it may not continue to spread throughout your body, it doesn't mean that damage hasn't been done. While the physical acts of abuse were not being committed, the mental pictures were constantly plaguing her mind on a daily basis. In essence, the mind becomes a mental torture chamber, in which the client sees no end and no hope. The cycle of negative thoughts followed by negative effects leading to hopelessness often cause a client to take drastic steps to find relief.

Attempts toward relief of mental suffering are numerous. I've seen clients use shopping, food, credit cards, alcohol, prescription drugs, illegal drugs, cutting, burning, or other self-harming behaviors in an attempt to gain "control" over an "out of control" mind. As you might imagine, none of these attempts will provide a permanent solution to the mental anguish. They only serve to compound a very complex problem and increase the negativity associated with the trauma.

One needs to remember that Katie has a diagnosis of PTSD. Flashbacks are a key to understanding how the client can become increasingly unstable when no active abuse is occurring. When flashbacks occur inside the minds of my clients, they describe it as though the event is literally happening to them with all their senses engaged and their person unplugged from reality. In other words, the active abuse is happening all over again, at least in their minds.

Katie once told me that almost every time she had sex with her husband, she would have flashbacks. These flashbacks consisted of both images of abuse and associated sensory feelings as well. As a result, Katie found herself being paralyzed by fear. She felt helpless, as she could not control her mind in what she was feeling and seeing during sex. Katie reported, "I felt really lost. I knew the way I was supposed to feel, but I couldn't. I couldn't seem to control the negative thoughts, even though I knew they were abnormal. It's so hard to not be able to control your feelings and your body. I couldn't allow myself to feel good about sex because I was constantly thinking to myself, 'This is wrong.'"

A doctor I had learned to trust recommended a trauma therapist. When I started seeing her, I had already begun a narrative of what I had experienced in my life. When she discovered how deep my wounds were, she recommended more concentrated help. She suggested that I agree to institutionalize myself. She wanted to send me to an out of state center that specialized in trauma. My insurance would not pay for that type of specialized care. Two mental health centers were the only two options that remained. One of my fears about being admitted was that I might not ever be allowed to leave. I felt that the inside of my mind was so crazy that when the professionals saw it, I would never be able to leave.

I asked Katie if she agreed with the therapist's idea of being admitted. She told me, "I was so messed up in my mind that I trusted the counselor to make the right decision for me." Notice how dependent and vulnerable Katie was at this point in her life. The counselor thought getting a lot of help in a short period of time would be best for Katie. Having someone admitted is a

major decision that should have involved many other
professionals. The only professional that was consulted was
Katie's medical doctor, who agreed. This decision would only
lead to Katie being further traumatized.

Once a facility was selected, I made the voluntary decision to admit myself. It was a Monday morning when I admitted myself. No one was allowed to have cell phones, toiletries, or food. Everything was locked up and down. The registration process lasted into the night. The intake process alone was traumatic. They made me stay in a room without a phone or anyone else in it. A lady interviewed me, but she left for lunch while I was supposed to meet with a new intake lady. I was in the room by myself for two hours while my husband was worried about me in the waiting room. I was told that if I left the room, my intake would be invalid.

Finally, my husband demanded to see me, and the staff realized that they had forgotten me. This was not surprising, as I seem to be forgotten a lot. They finally completed my intake. It took from 9:00 in the morning until 4:30 a.m. to get me checked in. After taking all my clothes off, a female worker patted me down. It was one of the most horrible things I've ever experienced. I had no choice about the person touching me. I had to do it. I felt less than human.

The first night, there was no visit from the psychiatrist, and subsequently, I had no medication. Another girl was in the room with me. We were not allowed to shut or lock the doors. This terrified me because we were being housed in a unit that had men. Every hour someone would check to see if we were in bed. The first night I did not sleep at all. The next day, I met with the psychiatrist. He reviewed the notes my therapist had sent with me.

After reviewing my case, the psychiatrist said he didn't feel like I belonged there because the treatment was tailored toward addiction counseling. He prescribed sleep and anxiety medication. Afterward, I went to the group therapy, but it was geared toward drug rehabilitation.

During one of the group sessions, I began to cry because everyone was talking about forgiving others and moving on. I kept asking the question, "How can a person deserve to be forgiven when they've done such terrible things?" It didn't seem rational to just forgive and move on. I was not okay with what they were saying, and no one seemed to be able to answer any of my "how to" questions. One of therapists took me into her office and told me that because of what I had gone through, I didn't have to forgive my abusers. Her words made me mad and confused. She didn't try to help answer any of my concerns. This made me feel dumb because I couldn't make her understand my point of view.

I was at the facility for three days. During that time, there was no one-on-one therapy offered. My hope was that intense therapy for a brief period of time would be given so I could get some relief from the suffering. This is what my therapist had told me. None was offered. All of the residents had a common bond in that they were all addicts. I wasn't and had nothing in common with them. During group sessions, I heard many of the residents talk about the need to forgive before they could move forward in their lives. This only created greater feelings of loneliness and isolation. On Thursday of that week, I was considered by the staff to be in stable condition and discharged.

What disappointed me was that my therapist had supposedly researched this place and felt that it was going to help me. I was overcome by feelings of hopelessness and isolation. If that was to be the place to help me and they couldn't, then what hope did I ever have of getting any better? Actually, going to that facility made things worse. The entire time I was in that place I was terrified. Not to mention that this experience is now on my permanent health record. People look at you differently when they know you've been admitted to a mental hospital. For me, it was a total waste of time.

Katie desperately wanted help with her problems. Having spent so much time with her, I have come to understand that many of the counselors simply did not know what to do to help her and were not trained or equipped to deal with complex PTSD. At their core, I believe most counselors to be kind-hearted, good, and willing helpers. However, in Katie's life, some of her counselors should have provided a referral. A referral becomes necessary when counselors realize that they are not qualified to help a person due to the magnitude of the problem.

Unfortunately, the counselors oftentimes would simply stop the process or tell her that they couldn't do anything else to help. What should have happened was the counselor should have helped Katie find a more qualified counselor that could specifically address her situation. Sadly, the decision to find another counselor was left up to Katie.

For much of Katie's life, she has had a very fragile personality. This fragility led to her frustrations with counselors and inhibited her following through to find another counselor to replace those who were unable to help. When Katie first came to me for help, I was totally unaware of the depth and scope of her problems. I will admit that, like many of her former counselors, I found myself unprepared to help her with deep-seated difficulties.

Chapter 9

Out of the Shadows

Not long after graduating from my university, I started attending a very loving and open-minded church. Most of the people who attended were very welcoming and kind to me. My personality didn't really lend itself to getting to know very many people. It's hard to interact with people when your mind tells you that you should be afraid of them. I was feeling frustrated and confused and wanted answers about God. At this point in my life, I was very angry at the world. There was so much about life, family, and people that I did not understand. The world for me was a very confusing place, full of questions with no apparent answers. It felt as though I had no control over anything in my life.

One of the main things that kept creeping up in my life was

the subject of forgiveness. While in group therapy at the mental hospital, many people had talked about the importance of forgiving others before they had been able move forward in their lives. Listening to their stories had only fueled my anger that I had not been able to forgive and move forward. As a result of constantly being so frustrated, I became passionate about finding answers as to how I might accomplish this in my personal life.

One evening, I was at church by myself, which is a rarity. I decided to ask Dr. Paul Helton, who is a licensed counselor, about forgiveness. It is not something I would normally do, but I felt compelled that day. I was extremely nervous about approaching Dr. Helton, but I was very determined to find answers to my questions. My mind works slowly in conversation because I tend to overthink issues and my mind splinters into a million pieces. So, to ask anyone a question is difficult. To ask the deeper questions concerning human actions and forgiveness produced a higher amount of anxiety than normal.

I explained that I was having trouble forgiving some people who wronged me and as a result, I felt like a failure as a Christian. We couldn't talk in depth that night, so we set up another meeting to discuss it further. When we met, I briefly said that I had been hurt, was unable to talk about it, and was trying to figure things out. He said that he wanted to help me. I explained that I had been in therapy for years and had been receiving weekly counseling for six months. He felt that I should have made more progress by now. As frustrated as I was with counselors, I agreed with his analysis. I still wasn't convinced that any counselor could be trusted to actually help me.

As a therapist, he believed he could help me. I have had very few people to reach out to me in hopes of helping me become better. I have had understanding people that felt bad for me and wanted me better but didn't know what to do to fix me. It surprised me. I had a therapist, and I wasn't looking for therapy. I don't know what I was looking for, maybe a miracle. I actually was warned against seeking therapy with him because of his reputation for intense therapy. One of my friends had sought his help, which had served beneficial for my friend. However, she told me that he was very straightforward in his approach to treatment.

Dr. Helton was confident that whatever I had been struggling with, he could help me with hopes of me being better within a few months. So, I said I would think about it. The whole concept kind of made me nervous, to be in therapy with someone that you see on a regular basis. Let's just say, I had my doubts. I talked it over with my husband. We both thought it was a good idea since I wasn't happy with the therapist I was seeing. I felt that she had handed me off to the mental institution because she couldn't deal with me.

Before the first official meeting with Dr. Helton, I was scared. My greatest fear was that he, like so many other counselors, wouldn't believe me. I was terrified of being alone with him. I was afraid he would hurt me. To be honest, I don't remember what we talked about in our first meeting. I do recall we filled out a good bit of paperwork. Once he realized my fear and the failure of other counselors, he offered for his wife to be present in the same room to help make me more comfortable. Her presence did help me feel more comfortable.

Due to the difficulty of being unable to verbalize my history, I asked Dr. Helton if I could just write it all down and let him read it. He said, "Absolutely." I was so relieved. Therapy for me was so stressful. I could hardly make any words come out of my mouth. I was scared of Dr. Helton not believing me and telling me it was my fault and that I deserved it. In reality, I felt he would see me as less than human. My fear was stifling.

After I gave him my journal, I was so nervous about what he would think about me. I remember he called me at 10:30 p.m. one night and told me he had just finished reading my journal. The first question I asked him was, "So, you don't hate me?" He said, "How could I hate you? You haven't done anything wrong." He told me he hated the things that had happened to me. He promised that he would do everything in his power to help me. He said, "I will make a vow to never quit, unless I die, until you are better." I never felt hope like I did at that moment.

Reading Katie's journal was one of the most difficult things I've ever done. Paragraph after paragraph of pain, suffering, torture, and the most humiliating trauma I had ever seen. Like many people, my reaction was one of sadness. When I called her to express my sentiments, I was taken back by her question, "So you don't hate me?" That night, I did not realize the gravity of that particular question. I do recall thinking, "what a strange question to ask."

In the coming sessions, I would begin to understand why Katie would ask about me hating her. For most of her life, she had felt unworthy and that much of what had happened to her was somehow her fault. In truth, none of it was her fault, but she did not perceive her life that way. Perception would become one of our biggest obstacles in therapy. Helping Katie to understand and believe that these events were not her fault and that she was innocent was very difficult. One might assume that Katie would be so tired of feeling bad that this would be welcomed news. Not the case. Her core beliefs were so ingrained that she was bad and to be blamed that hearing anything different was almost intolerable. It would be well over a year before she would be open to even allowing herself to entertain ideas relating to her innocence.

For therapists who may be considering taking on clients with trauma, I would ask that you think about a few things. First, do you have the training necessary to help the client? If not, you will be doing them a service by helping them find someone who is better suited for them. Believe me when I say, I know how hard it can be to admit that you are not qualified to help a client. However, try not to allow your willingness to supersede your abilities. Second, I would encourage therapists to think long-term. Most of my clients are with me for a few weeks, get to doing better, and are discharged. This was not to be the case with Katie. Now, I have a much better understanding of how important it is to consider long-term relationships with trauma clients a must. Third, if you are considering engaging in the difficult work of treating trauma patients, then get the proper training. There are many approaches available with positive outcome data. It is time-consuming and often costly, but it is a key to working with and successfully treating trauma victims.

Chapter 10

Long and Winding Road

This chapter includes our thoughts on what was taking place in our minds during some of our sessions. In all of my years of counseling, only one case comes to mind that would even compare to the immensity of pain and suffering Katie had endured. I say that, not to diminish other cases in which people suffer, but to point out that this case was different from the very start. What started out as a discussion on forgiveness developed into a counseling relationship and a dynamic, tiring, and extremely painful journey for both of us.

Our first meeting was awkward and uneasy. Katie said that she wanted to ask me some questions about prayer and forgiveness. The discussion proceeded as I attempted to answer her questions. At some point in the conversation I asked, "How *have you been wronged?" That created a very aversive reaction on her part. She quickly dropped her head and went completely silent. I was taken back by her response, especially since she had initiated the conversation. Suddenly, she wasn't talking or making any eye contact. Her reaction was the picture of defeat, agony and utter devastation. Never before or since have I seen such a reaction to a simple question.*

What I thought to be a basic question about wrongdoing opened a world of pain I had not expected. The sexual, physical, emotional, and spiritual abuse Katie had endured was so traumatic the question silenced her completely. This event has changed how I approach and handle situations involving abuse. For example, if you are dealing with someone you suspect has been traumatized, ask the person if she would prefer to write her thoughts in a journal for you to read. Asking Katie for details was creating such overwhelming flashbacks, she was unable to verbally communicate. To avoid re-traumatizing a client, the journal is an excellent alternative.

Read one of Katie's journal entries and consider the inner workings of her mind:

My dreams have changed. There is a girl watching them do things to me and telling me how I deserve it or that I am a bad person. I always had these thoughts pop into my head. Phrases like "I hate her," or "I want to kill her." When I thought about the abuse, I always thought about what "they" did to me, even if it was just my brother. She was always there, and that girl was me.

The little girl is inside me sometimes; I ignore her. Sometimes I hate her. Sometimes I *am* her. I pretend she is not there. I hate her because she was there when they hurt me. She was there telling them to punish me because I was bad. Sometimes she is still there. When I walk into a room, I find a safe place. A place I can go when I am scared. I see myself curled in a ball there.

The fractured mind is a torture chamber. The victim feels trapped, hopeless, and broken inside her mind. As we worked through event after event, Katie would begin to develop skills that would allow her to calm her fears. These skills would unlock the door to her mind and free her to find her voice and her identity. Although it is freeing to be delivered from the ghosts of the past, one is now faced with new difficulties. One of the most trying difficulties is finding oneself not knowing how to proceed with this newfound freedom to think for oneself. The victims are challenged to make decisions for themselves. This is unfamiliar territory, and often confusing. Throughout our therapy, finding her voice and identity were two of Katie's greatest struggles.

The reason I sought you (Dr. Helton) out was more for spiritual help than anything. After leaving the mental hospital, I felt so messed up. All my efforts to "get better" were not working. Inside I felt so broken. I began to believe that I couldn't be fixed. Daily I was tormented by the feeling of dread that I would be stuck in the past. Being a person with an individual personality was a foreign concept to me. I wanted to be normal. The problem is that I couldn't figure out the meaning of normal. I felt like I had no hope on this earth, and I was trying to figure out my beliefs about God.

For many clients who have suffered abuse, the lack of hope is a core issue for treatment. Often the client can be locked into a psychological loop that suppresses any positive thoughts that lead to hopeful thinking. That certainly was the case for Katie. In fact, at this point in her life she had become so accustomed to being in a state of hopelessness that she was grasping for a reason to keep living.

I wanted to be able to forgive those who wronged me, but I didn't know how.

Something inside me has to believe that Katie was seeking help for many reasons. Prior to our therapy, the counseling process had been so unsuccessful that she stopped seeking clinical help and started seeking spiritual counsel. Her choice did not mean she didn't need professional help, only that it had not been successful up to that point in her life.

When we started meeting together, I wanted so badly to get better. I trusted you when you said you were going to help me.

For months, Katie did not reveal that she trusted me. She was so quiet and timid she could barely respond to any questions or thoughts concerning her abuse and abusers. Counselors must often press on despite the lack of outward signs of success, in hopes that the therapeutic relationship will grow and yield a positive outcome. It was very hard to determine if the therapeutic process was working or not. Now that I know what she was feeling, it is much easier to understand clients that may not be responding in a way that acknowledges their trust is growing. The process was slowly working, even though the visible signs were not evident. Reassuring a client that they are growing is an indispensible therapeutic tool. Use it often.

At this point I want to give the reader some ideas behind the primary tool I was utilizing in Cognitive Behavioral Therapy. The National Association of Cognitive Behavioral Therapists states that,

"Cognitive-Behavioral Therapy...is a form of psychotherapy that emphasizes the important role of thinking in how we feel and what we do. Cognitive-behavioral therapy does not exist as a distinct therapeutic technique. The term "cognitive-behavioral therapy (CBT)" is a very general term for a classification of therapies with similarities. There are several approaches to cognitive-behavioral therapy, including Rational Emotive Behavior Therapy, Rational Behavior Therapy, Rational Living Therapy, Cognitive Therapy, and Dialectic Behavior Therapy."

http://www.nacbt.org/whatiscbt.htm

The National Alliance of Mental Illness states that, "Cognitive-behavioral therapy (CBT) focuses on exploring relationships among a person's thoughts, feelings, and behaviors. During CBT, a therapist will actively work with a person to uncover unhealthy patterns of thought and how they may be causing self-destructive behaviors and beliefs.

By addressing these patterns, the person and therapist can work together to develop constructive ways of thinking that will produce healthier behaviors and beliefs. For instance, CBT can help someone replace thoughts that lead to low self-esteem ("I can't do anything right") with positive expectations ("I can do this most of the time, based on my prior experiences").

The core principles of CBT are identifying negative or false beliefs and testing or restructuring them. Oftentimes, someone being treated with CBT will have homework in between sessions where they practice replacing negative thoughts with more realistic thoughts based on prior experiences, or record their negative thoughts in a journal." https://www.nami.org/Learn-More/Treatment/Psychotherapy#sthash.QRbeLg1t.dpuf

For numerous articles on Cognitive-Behavioral Therapy, you can visit the National Institute of Mental Health Website https://www.nimh.nih.gov/search.jsp?query=cognitive+behavioral+therapy

We would meet for a session, and it would last three or four hours, with me only saying a few words. Any time you would ask me a question, I would totally shut down. My brain couldn't handle it. You would ask me a simple question about what happened to me, and all the abuse would run through my head. And not just thoughts - I would be thrown back to when it was happening to me.

On one occasion I remember Katie saying, "When you ask me a question, it's like you throw a bomb into my head, and my mind goes into a thousand pieces." I did not realize the magnitude of her pain and despair. Her trouble responding was directly related to being overwhelmed with the initial thought and quickly being filled with anxiety. In later sessions, it would become clear that she was experiencing PTSD flashbacks. I would tell her that these flashbacks are when the past becomes the present. When this happens, there is a flooding of emotions that shut down a client's ability to think through the questions and respond appropriately. These flashbacks became one of the greatest enemies to her progress. Katie was totally shutting down emotionally and being immobilized by the PTSD into silence.

But I loved listening to you talk. Everything you said made me think. You made me think about who I could be if I let myself. You believed in me when I didn't. I wanted to change so badly. I was trying so hard. Every time I went to talk to you, I would try to calm myself. I would try to force myself to say things. Even those three or four words I said took so much for me to say.

Although I did not see the visible signs of change, I believed Katie could become more whole as a person. The abuse had so damaged her confidence, self-esteem, and person that she was unable to communicate what little change was taking place. My promise to her to not quit was often the driving force behind me forging ahead with no end in sight.

When I left from our sessions, I felt so defeated. You were

doing everything you could to help me, but I was failing. I wouldn't quit because if I quit coming to see you I would have to quit life itself, because for me, this was it. I had tried everything I knew to become a better person, to become a whole person.

There were so many nights I would watch as Katie walked to her car with shoulders drooped and head hung low. Not wanting to be negative, I would try to encourage her with whatever words seemed appropriate in the moment. At the conclusion of most sessions, I shut the door utterly exhausted. I can only imagine what Katie felt as she drove home.

I remember when you tried to hypnotize me, and it didn't work. I actually talked to you more that day than I previously had. I was so disappointed in myself that I couldn't do it. I had the same feeling of frustration when we first started EMDR, and I couldn't do that either.

Time will not allow me to fully discuss the nature of being unsuccessful in her attempts to communicate or cooperate with hypnosis. Her depression increased as she was unable to talk, process feelings, or engage in sessions. I had to find another way to treat her. The direction we were headed was simply not going to move her toward a positive outcome. Clearly, the treatment was not effective enough to move her toward better mental health.

There had been improvements in the reduction of self-harming behaviors and her increased ability to talk, although not as much as she wanted. Something else had to be tried to help her in a more forward. Having made the promise to Katie that I would not give up on her, I felt I must seek an alternative to Cognitive-Behavioral Therapy, Guided Imagery, and Relaxation Techniques.

After spending many months working with Katie with very little success, I made the decision to conduct hypnosis. During my years of working with trauma victims, I have found this treatment to be extremely effective. The process was discussed, and the time and date was selected to utilize hypnosis. From the outset, I had very high hopes that this would help to move Katie into a better place in her mind and heart.

The evening came, and we began what is known as the initial induction into relaxation. Music is regularly used to assist the client with relaxation. Within minutes, it was obvious that Katie was not going to be able to relax enough to concentrate on moving to the next step, which is age regression. Unfortunately, the session ended not long after it had begun. Within moments, my heart sank as I had hoped that this technique would help her at so many levels. Quite the opposite occurred. Katie was disappointed in herself. I tried to assure her that it was not her fault. As our evening concluded and Katie left, I was discouraged. Hypnosis has been my main "go to" technique. Suddenly, I was facing a client who experienced no benefits from hypnosis. Up to that point in my career, this technique had always worked for clients. For me, it was a rude awakening. My promise to Katie not to give up on her would motivate me to drive forward to find a technique that might help turn the tide.

That night, I knew I had to find some other options that would be effective in treating the issues surrounding complex PTSD. As her clinician, I had exhausted my ideas and treatment options, feeling great disappointment. As I began to research effective treatment options for severely traumatized patients, I kept seeing a recurring treatment option: EMDR. The further I probed, the more articles began to surface explaining the method and the effective treatment outcomes with patients. Interestingly, the results were coming from many different populations of people crossing gender and cultures accordingly. This was the encouragement for which I had been searching. The research findings on EMDR created hope in my spirit. Was this the answer to a breakthrough? One could only hope.

Some months before, I had attended a continuing education seminar, and I met a woman who was certified to administer EMDR. After locating her business card, I made contact with her and asked for help in locating an EMDR trainer. The closest trainer to me was Dr. Ed Hurley in Clarksville, Tennessee. Dr. Hurley was a retired officer from the Army where he had served as a chaplain. He possessed extensive knowledge in trauma, war, casualty, and grief, due in large part to his military career. For me, his extensive knowledge and training made him an obvious choice.

Once enrolled for my training, I continued reading and researching to better understand this technique. I wanted to know the history, theory, techniques, and treatment outcomes before attending the training. Time did not allow me to digest the vast amount of material that exists on the subject before attending my first day of class. For those of you who are clinicians, please do your homework on techniques. Old habits may cause you to "stick with" a technique that may not be working for your client. There are times to scrap what is not working and find other treatment options. Had I not been willing to do that, I would have become Katie's fifth counselor to give up on her. That was not going to happen.

The "Basic Training" course for EMDR takes place over a period of three weekends, a total of seven, eight-hour days of training. Within days after completing the training, I was ready to utilize EMDR. Although I was ready to begin the treatment, Katie struggled to "stay connected" during the sets of bi-lateral stimulation. One of her difficulties was trying to process an image without disassociating. She had become so accustomed to "vanishing" when confronted by active trauma, that the idea of thinking about an image of the specific trauma would trigger her into a dissociative state.

At that point, we began intensive work on Mindfulness. This consisted of numerous exercises to assist with the integration of mind and body. In other words, teaching her mind to be present in her body. Allowing her to learn how to engage her mind with her body would become the foundation for her sessions of EMDR. Now, I ask my clients who choose EMDR to practice at least three *mindful exercises a day in between sessions.*

After extensive practice in mindfulness everyday for three weeks, Katie returned and the EMDR sessions resumed. For the first time since beginning therapy with Katie, which at that point had been a year and a half, we were having "major" breakthroughs with reprocessing her painful memories. Over a two-week period, we had seven sessions and made more progress than a year and a half of talk therapy.

Those breakthroughs started to produce momentum in treatment like nothing we had seen up to that point. With each client, we begin with a 10/10 list. The client is asked to list 10 of the most positive things that have ever happened to them and 10 of the most negative things that have ever happened. The list of the 10 negatives is the treatment plan for the client. We begin treating the least painful memory first and work from that point.

As Katie's list of traumatic memories grew, so did our number of successful processing of each and every one of those events. With the help of EMDR, Katie would not "forget" what she had been through, but she would be able to recall those memories without shutting down and checking out. The negative effect of those painful memories would dissipate. Finally, the breakthrough for which both of us had been hoping!

I also remember the first time I successfully completed an EMDR session, and that really made everything worth it. It felt like a weight was lifted off my chest. I felt like that was my second beginning at life. My second chance to live.

Notice the last line you just read: "My second chance to live." EMDR provided Katie a second chance to live! The way of resistance was beginning to crumble. It was like a miracle had occurred overnight. Suddenly, we were able to process her events without her being completely overwhelmed. It was one of the most incredible treatments I had ever attempted.

For those therapists who are working with trauma patients, I suggest you consider adding EMDR to your techniques. Prior to my work with Katie, hypnosis had worked most effectively. With Katie, hypnosis showed no efficacy and was soon discarded as an ineffective treatment option.

I want to share a short note Katie to wrote me as her therapy progressed:

I wanted to thank you for everything you do for me. I wish I could actually tell you how much you mean to me. I am afraid if I tried I would start crying. So, for now, you will have to do with a letter. I think of you and Dana as family. Especially since I am probably staying away from my "real" family. You guys give me hope. I wouldn't be going forward without you. I would be burying myself further from God. I don't want to go home. I will miss you. Keep changing people's lives. They need you. I don't know what the future will hold for me. I know whatever I do, it will bring me pain. But I will always have hope of a better me because of you.

Both Katie and I felt relief at the "breakthrough" we had experienced. Relief is a word that comes to mind, but it doesn't seem to do justice to what we both felt. The first few sessions were so successful that it made Katie feel a bit uneasy. It was like she was afraid to be optimistic. She feared being unable to continue being so successful in her communication and processing of events. It was also very hard for her to "feel." When being abused, a person is often told what they should feel or think. Now, she was being given the freedom to decide for herself what to feel. Time would reveal that success was not only possible, but it was going to be a regular part of our sessions.

Many of my EMDR clients have similar reactions to Katie. For years, they have believed it was "wrong" to feel good about the most basic aspects of life, like being married or having children. Feeling good for someone who has suffered abuse can be a very scary feeling. After a few sessions of EMDR, I find my clients have more "mental room" for healthy emotions and begin to become more comfortable with feeling good making their own choices of what to feel and how to respond to people.

Chapter 11

Making Sense Out Of Non-Sense

About a year and a half into therapy Katie asked me the question, "Do you think I should write my parents a letter?" This is a very normal question for a survivor to ask a therapist. It took Katie a long time before she would even allow herself to think about it, much less talk to me about it. We discussed the possibility for a while, and I simply asked her, "Why would you want to do that?" I tried not to direct her one way or the other, but I asked her to weigh the possible outcomes. After many months, she said she thought she was going to write them. That evening, we spent hours talking about what she might say. The discussion included: to whom she might write first, time intervals, or whether to send all of the letters at once.

I suggest to fellow therapists that if a client approaches you with this type question that you be the "guide on the side." Allow them to take the lead and make the decision for themselves. It was difficult to think about all of the scenarios that could result from such letters. Her family is unpredictable, which complicated writing to them even more.

It might be easy, while helping someone like Katie, to have the urge to step in and help her make the decision. My encouragement would be not to overstep your boundary as a helper. It is vital that the victim come to a resolved decision in her own mind. Katie would agonize over this decision. Second guessing herself is common. Katie would ask me several, "What if...." questions. In my view, these questions can be part of the therapeutic purging process. For Katie, writing these letters was very painful. Waiting for a response after sending these kinds of letters was excruciating. Below you can read her thoughts.

All my life I never believed that my parents or other family members could ever say anything that would make me understand why they did the things they did to me. The thought of writing letters to my family expressing my thoughts never seemed to be a good option. I guess I felt that if I didn't approach them about the past, I wouldn't have to face their responses. After a great deal of time in therapy and self-reflection, I made the decision to write my family members individual letters.

The first letter I drafted was for my dad. I remember feeling that I knew what my dad had done to me. I wasn't sure if my mom knew about the abuse. So, I made the decision to write to my father first. After I finished the letter, I asked Dr. Helton to read it and tell me what he thought. Here's the letter I gave him to read.

Letter #1 – To My dad

I hate you. I really, really hate you. I hate that because of you all my childhood memories are horrible. You hurt me so much. You broke me. It sucks that the first memory I have is of you molesting me. When I think of you, I feel sick. I don't want to be around you. I don't even want to write you this letter. I wish you weren't my father. I want you to go away and not come back. You are a sick and evil person. The first person I had sex with is my father. That is so disgusting. I hate that there is this huge part of me that I have to cut out and now it feels like there is nothing left. I hate that you haunt my dreams. I am tired of being strong. Because of you I could never let go and be free. I just want to melt away. Thank God I am stubborn or I would probably be dead by now. You made it impossible for me to live. Oh, I survived. But never lived. I had to die inside because the pain was too great. I am selfish enough to want you to be in Heaven because it is the only way that I would know you are sorry for what you did. That you asked for forgiveness for the evil you did against me. One day I hope I can forgive you, but right now I can't. I just can't.

After reading the letter Dr. Helton and I discussed the pros and cons of sending it. We deliberated and I made the decision not to send it and redraft another letter. I felt as though the language might be more than my dad was capable of handling. I didn't want the language to be so abrasive that he would shut down, even though all of it was true. My hope was that he would be open to my confrontation of his actions.

Below are the three letters I wrote and mailed to my dad, mom and brother.

Letter #2 – To My Dad

I don't know how to start this letter. I don't know what to call you. Dad? Because that term is a term of endearment, and that is not a quality you possess. Actually, when I think about you, I want to throw up. I don't know what to say to you. I don't know if words can describe my feelings. It almost seems silly to even ask THE QUESTION: Why did you molest me? Because there is no answer that could possibly make sense or make me feel better. It is something I will never understand. I would rather die than hurt my children like you hurt me. So, let's skip the whys and go to the real question I have. Are you sorry for what you did? Are you sorry for stealing my childhood? I didn't have a chance to be innocent and carefree. I was always scared, scared of you. Are you sorry for turning your shame into my shame? Your evil into my evil? I thought there was something wrong with me. Are you sorry for all the beatings you gave me for being shy and not talking to people? I was afraid to open my mouth because of the secrets I had locked inside. I was just a kid, and I was protecting you. All I wanted was to be loved. That was your job. Now I am scared of love. Afraid that love and pain will always be connected. I hate what you did to me. It will always be with me, and I will always hate it. But I am stronger than you. You stole my childhood, but not my life. Because of you I am a stronger person and a better parent than you can hope to be. The End.

I remember the night I wrote this letter, I cried until I eventually fell asleep.

The letters make great material to be utilized during counseling sessions. These letters allowed me to explore Katie's deeper feelings that were tied to her expressions she had written. For many clients, like Katie, it is far easier to write their feelings pertaining to their trauma than to actually verbalize the trauma. Early on in therapy we learned that writing was going to be one of the most successful tools for allowing Katie to express her deep-seated pain.

Letter #3 – To My Mom

I have some questions I need you to answer. Did you know that Dad, _____, and _____ sexually abused me? Part of me feels like, "How could you not know?" Maybe you wanted to deny the facts because it was too hard to face. Here are the things that I remember that you should have figured out but chose not to see. When I was four, I stopped hugging and kissing anyone. I couldn't stand physical contact with people. I know you noticed because I remember hearing you try to explain it away to people. I never told you I loved you until I was in college. Not even in response to you saying it to me. Weird, right? How about all the bladder and yeast infections I would get as a kid? We were at the doctor's office all the time. How about the fact that I would wet my pants at home all the time? I slept on your floor until I was fourteen because I was scared and had nightmares. What about all the times I would wake up and throw up in the middle of the night but was fine the next day? Coincidence? The only reason I stopped sleeping in your room was because I begged you to get me a bunk bed. You know what teenager wants bunk beds? One that isn't safe on the ground. Remember when my brother kicked me in the crotch so hard it bruised me, and I actually told you? You know what you said? You told me I probably deserved it. What was wrong with you? I understand wanting to protect your child, protect your family. I did it for years. But I did it with only myself to sacrifice. You sacrificed me. You helped hurt me by "not knowing." Was it worth it? Save the family, but lose a child? Because that is what I am right now. Lost. I am slowly clawing my way back to living, but I might choose to always be lost to you. I might choose to not be close to you because of what you decided to do. I want to be strong and forgive you, but like I said, I am not whole yet so I can't. Maybe one day, but not today.

Letter #4 – Letter To My Brother

Dear Brother,

I wrote you this letter because I couldn't keep it a secret anymore. It was hurting too much inside. What you and my cousins did to me was wrong. I know you probably thought you were just messing around with me, but what you did to me was sexual abuse. You hurt me so badly. You ruined my childhood. I didn't have a chance to be normal because you were always there trying to hurt me. Everyday I have to think about what you did. You messed up my relationship with my husband, children, and my own self. I know I am supposed to forgive you, and I'm trying. But it is really hard. Maybe one day I can, but right now it is too painful.

After much discussion and thought, Katie sent these letters. For quite some time there was a great deal of anxiety on her part. She spent a great deal of time second-guessing her self. Was she doing the "right" thing? Would her family disown her? Or worse. Would they say she had made the whole story up and none of it was true? All of these questions were part of Katie's inner struggle to make some sense of why her family had been so cruel.

After she posted the letters, we would talk daily by phone and text. Neither of us knew the outcome. Waiting is agonizing. Those days of waiting for some response were filled with anxiety. There was little I could do other than offer words of encouragement. Finally, the response came.

Her father's response was to say, "I don't see where talking about it is going to help anything." Her mother booked a flight and made a special visit to Katie's home and claimed she knew nothing about all the years of abuse and said she was "so sorry." If her mother's response had been true, that would have offered some small consolation. However, because of details I will not reveal, both Katie and I believe, with certainty, her mother was lying. She knew what was happening to Katie and did nothing to stop the abuse. Her brother would offer a half-hearted email apology.

Needless to say, Katie was devastated by the lack of sincere regret and remorse from her family. Their response prompted Katie to begin to think about how she was going to proceed in her interactions with them from this point forward. Her family's responses caused Katie to question how she should respond to them. Should she just "say no more?" It certainly appeared her family wanted to have no more conversations about the matter. Should she continue to push for an apology? How about "waiting them out" to see if they will come to her with a sincere apology? These were just a few of the dilemmas we would discuss in treatment. At this point, Katie believes her family should acknowledge their wrongs before healing between them can take place. I agree.

After much deliberation, Katie decided to write a response to her parents. Before making the decision to send the letter, we discussed possible outcomes. My interest was to help her decide for herself what she wanted to do; not make the decision for her. One reason for giving her ample space to decide was there would be certain consequences, which had the potential to be devastating.

The therapist needs to prepare trauma victims for the worst possible scenario. Failure to do so should be considered unethical. In our discussions, I did not hold back the reality that her family might not even respond to her, might call her a liar, or even deny all of her accusations. When a family has kept "secrets" for years, the family dynamic is so dysfunctional that to introduce truth can be crushing to all guilty parties. So often, families desperately want to be "left alone" and "pretend" as though nothing has ever happened. Such had been the case with Katie's family.

Imagine what holidays were like for Katie. Having to return to the same house where she had been abused. All the sights, sounds, and smells that would trigger the emotional pain and mental trauma. Think about her sitting at the Thanksgiving or Christmas table and looking across to see those who had tortured her and robbed her of the innocence of her childhood. It's a wonder she was able to attend those gatherings and function with some sense of normalcy.

Katie told me that she would always have an impending dread that would come over her before returning home for the holidays. Panic attacks were constant. She told me, "Everything is connected to memory." Therefore, while she was in the house where she was abused, she had great difficulty sleeping. Although she attempted to sleep in her "old room", she couldn't sleep there. "I had to sleep in the front room," she would tell me.

Words cannot describe the courage it took for Katie to write this letter. Think of the risks she took. Most of us seldom have to draw on our emotional reserves in order to confront our fears.

Time after time, Katie has boldly moved forward with her
recovery. Although she experienced immense emotional pain at
her family's failure to respond in a loving and restorative way, she
moved forward nonetheless. Next, you will read the letter to her
Mom and Dad.

It really hurt how you handled me confronting your role in my abuse. You basically ignored what I said and didn't want to talk about how I felt. Mom, it was a lie for you to say you didn't know what was happening. If you are going to lie and pretend it didn't happen, then I'm not sure I want you around my children. I already don't trust you to be alone with them, but I feel like I shouldn't trust you at all. Also, if you want to continue to have a relationship with my family, you cannot encourage my children to keep secrets from me. When you say, "we won't tell your mom," and you tell me anyway, it teaches them to not trust adults. This might not faze you, but it is important to me that my children love and trust me.

Dad, to tell me you are sorry and do not want me to discuss what happened any further is another way to control me and to control the situation, and that is not going to happen. I am not a little girl you can trick and use with no consequences. I feel like you aren't really sorry that you really hurt me, and you are more sorry that I wouldn't keep your secret. You tried to make it all about (brother's name) and ignore your role in what happened. I want to be able to talk about my feelings of what happened without being shut down. I'm trying to forgive you for what you have done, but having you not seem to care is making it very difficult for me to find forgiveness. If you feel you want to right the wrongs and not just shut me up, feel free to contact me, but until then, please leave me alone.

Katie would call me after she had already mailed the letter you just read. My first response was, "You're awesome!" I was so proud of her resolve in sending those heartfelt words that tore through her heart. That strength demonstrates her determination to move forward with her own personal recovery. Frequently, I tell Katie how honored I am to be in the same room as her. It's not just counselors who are the helpers. Katie has and continues to be a constant source of encouragement to my family and me. She is an amazing human being.

For many days we both waited in anxious anticipation of her family's response. It was apparent that Katie desperately hoped that in some way her family would acknowledge their wrongs, ask for her forgiveness, and ask for a second chance. Both of us realized that might be too much to hope for. Unfortunately, the only response that would come was in a phone call from her mother.

Katie sent me a text letting me know what she thought about her mother. Her language was very plain. This alerted me to the fact that contact had been made, and it did not appear to have gone well. Immediately, I called Katie only to be met with a fragile and extremely sad voice on the other end of the phone. Finally, she spoke and said, "All my mom could say is, "How could you ruin our family like this?" Katie was devastated. I grieved for her.

After talking for a few moments, I asked Katie this question, "You're not gonna let them win, are you?" She responded with a definitive, "No!" From that point on, the conversation took a more positive direction. Later that evening, I placed a follow up call to Katie and talked with her for some time about moving forward. During that call, her mood became lighter, and she seemed more refreshed. Katie sent me a text that said, "Thanks for calling me. It helped me to feel better." One thing I have learned is that it is vital that the counselor provide a foundation of support outside the office. Please don't accept trauma patients if you are not going to be available for them. Many hours will be needed outside the office to help win the day for your client, friend, or loved one.

Had Katie and I not worked through the possible negative outcomes prior to her sending those letters, this might have been a debilitating setback. Katie would tell me that this exercise of considering the worst possible outcomes helped her in processing the rejection that ultimately came from her family. Therapists should take note of the importance of adequately preparing their client for disappointment. Notice Katie's thoughts concerning the writing of these letters.

Writing the letters was one of the hardest things I have done. I had lived my whole life being confused of what was happening to me, to being scared that someone would find out. I always was told that if I let anyone know about my life, I would destroy our family. I already felt like being abused was my fault. In my mind, I couldn't handle being the sole destroyer of our family.

When I thought about writing my family, I still had the "I'm scared I will mess everything up" feelings. I was always taught to be obedient to my parents. You didn't argue or have your own opinion or you would suffer the consequences. I didn't expect my mom and dad or my brother and his wife to separate or anything like that, because divorce is not a viable option in my family. I had a feeling that I would have to bear the brunt of the bad feelings that would come from presenting the letters. I would have to be the peacemaker because that had always been my role. I thought there was a chance that they would turn against me. It seemed like a real possibility that my brother and father would join forces and deny their participation. It's hard to be hated, even if the fault isn't your own.

I can tell myself all day long that I am doing the right thing, but it still hurts to think that my family might not be on my side. No matter what, I am connected to these people. Yes, they did a crappy job raising me and not taking care of me, but they are still the people I love and depended on for a good portion of my life. It is hard to just stop the spark inside that is compelling you to love these people.

Waiting for a response from them was very tortuous. It was just not knowing what would happen that was the hardest part. I mean, I knew inside my head that there wasn't anything horrific that would happen to me. There was this stress of not knowing what would happen and knowing I would be the cause of everyone's stress. I have my natural daily stress and then all this extra pressure and it made me want to explode. I thought about cutting because cutting is always in the back of my mind. But I knew cutting was letting my family win, and I didn't want to allow that anymore.

The first response I got was from my mother. She texted me because I asked her not to call me because I was afraid I wouldn't be able to respond to her right away. She said that she got the letter. She said that she was sorry she didn't know what was happening to me. She said that she wanted to come and see me because she didn't want to text about it anymore. She came the next day and said that my dad was sorry. My mom said she was devastated for me. She cried and asked questions about what happened. How long did it happen? Where? When? I told her what I could without bombarding her with overwhelming details. That was the last time we talked about it.

The next day she acted like everything was the same, but to me the whole world seemed to change. Later, I received a text from my mom that said: "I don't know what to say to you. I go to your house to find out what happened and get basically nothing. I am stuck in the middle of people I love. I never knew any of this was going on. But somehow I am being put in the middle. But mostly I feel bad for your children. They are going to miss out on family things. They are old enough to know something's not right. You are the only one that can remedy this. Start with God, then go from there. Stop talking to everyone else, move on, and forgive."

At that point, I decided that I wasn't sure if my mother cared at all.

The more I talked about it, the less she wanted to hear. This was my first sense that my family wasn't really supportive. They were on damage control. It felt like it was almost better not knowing how they felt than knowing they really didn't care.

My brother's response I received via email. I was so angry when I read it, I deleted it. I didn't want to dwell on the negativity. I didn't want to keep going back to what he said and analyzing every detail of the email. He basically apologized that I was so hurt because of what he did to me. He didn't actually say he was sorry for doing it. I expected him to deny things.

People get good at telling themselves certain things didn't happen and that certain things are not the same because that is what they want to believe. That is their truth they devise. It was like my whole family was sorry they got caught. They put on these lying, "I'm glad you told" faces while they really resented that I refused to keep their secrets.

The second letter I wrote to my parents came with a different type of anxiety. They already knew about the abuse, so there was no surprise there. But, in this letter I had set boundaries. I wasn't going to let them push away what happened. It was a risk to boldly defy my parents. I knew there wasn't an option to back down. I also knew they had options, too. One being to decide they didn't want to be a part of my family anymore. The days after I sent the letter were torture not knowing how they would respond.

When my phone would ring, my heart felt like it was going to beat out of my throat. When my mother called, I couldn't sit still. I paced in a circle until I was dizzy trying to release some of the tension. She was crying and said that she didn't know why I was trying to ruin our family. She said she didn't know why I was putting her in between my dad and me. I said that it was her decision to be in the middle and that she had the option of being on my side. She said she couldn't do that. I told her I didn't want to talk to her anymore and hung up.

Why would I even want to forgive my parents? Why do I even want to have a relationship with them? I think it is a natural response to want to belong, to be a part of something that is supposed to be special. That is why we have families, so we are not alone. I think there is a need inside me to want my family to survive. My parents are not doing the right thing by denying their responsibility. A lot of people choose to be evil. It's easy to do the wrong thing. It is hard to want to give my family a second chance. It is hard to forgive them. But it is the right thing to do.

I want to be better than what they are. I want to try my best to be who they are not. When I get to Heaven, I don't want God to say, "Why did you give up so easily?" I want to know I tried my hardest to do the right thing.

For those who are struggling to recover from sexual trauma I would say the road can and oftentimes will be filled with many obstacles, hazards, and unanticipated setbacks. You may find that you have to push yourself to find the inner strength to deal with all the "family issues" that are sure to arise. Many families are not prepared for the family "secrets" to be unraveled. Denial becomes one of the most common responses.

Although others may choose poorly, it doesn't necessitate you doing the same. Katie did not bow to the immense pressure exerted by her family to "keep quiet." She purposefully chose to move forward, and you can too.

Chapter 12

Free To Feel...Again

It's hard to allow yourself to be free to feel. It's something that should be as simple as breathing, but you never really learned how to do it properly. At first, it really hurts. That's what I was afraid of when it came to feeling. I thought if I felt again, it would hurt so much I wouldn't be able to stand it. But you already have been through the hard part, the abuse. The feeling part will never hurt as much as the abuse. But it does hurt. Everything hurts. Everything seems to be tied to pain. You mourn so many things: loss of childhood, loss of innocence, and the loss of feeling itself. But then the pain begins to fade if you allow it. Then, a tiny piece of hope floats into your soul. And, if you grasp onto that hope, it will carry you to better places.

How did I learn to feel again? Slowly. I had to tell myself it was okay to feel. Sometimes I would sit on the floor and tell myself over and over again, "I'm okay. I'm going to be okay." Just because it hurts doesn't mean it is bad. I still struggle with holding my feelings inside. Sometimes I feel confused and frustrated because I don't know what I am feeling. Pain is the easiest to feel. It was the first thing I learned to push away and the first feeling to come back.

Anger and sadness were also some of the easier feelings. It's the "happy" feelings that are hard. They are so much harder to remember how to do. Sometimes I feel like if I am happy, something will break. It's hard to combine the feelings of safety and happiness. They don't seem to mix. Crying is still a struggle for me. The first time I really cried about what happened to me, I felt out of control, which was difficult for someone who exerts restraint. I felt like my sadness was controlling me.

Later, I figured out you could choose how you feel. It isn't something that pushes you. You guide it to where you want to go. Crying still doesn't feel that good, but I really don't think it is supposed to.

Having likes and dislikes: The toughest part of having an opinion is remembering that people are interested in what I have to say; that if I disagree, I won't get a punishment. It is difficult not knowing when people are just having a conversation. It's also more natural for me to know my dislikes than my likes. I can't seem to figure out what I like. I'm scared that if I admit I like something, it will be taken away from me. I'm working on letting go, figuring out that the good and the bad don't always have to be together. I have to convince myself that having opinions won't get me in trouble. I'm an adult who has choices. Other people aren't controlling me. I control myself.

The return to "feeling" was one of the most difficult parts of Katie's therapy. Many times she told me she felt guilty for feeling good. During her formative years, she was made to feel as though she was less than human. Her protection and security were removed from her life by her caregivers. This creates insecure attachment.

Research on attachment continues to help us understand that when a child does not begin life securely attached, the resulting insecurity may take a lifetime to recover. The doubts and self-talk become a way of life as they begin to find their way deep into a person's beliefs about themselves. Katie was bad, or so she thought. Her environment was the war zone, not her mind. However, one's environment is tied to one's self-concept and self-esteem. Sadly for Katie, the formative period of her young life was consumed with thoughts of her unworthiness. These unhealthy feelings dominated all aspects of her life.

The hardest part is allowing yourself to let go of the past and reach for something different. I used to not have a voice. I had no boundaries. I didn't feel like I was worth even having an opinion. If I disagreed with someone, it felt like I was betraying him or her.

Now, I have learned to be my own individual person with likes and dislikes. I have allowed myself to disagree with others, to stand up for things I believe. I used to be afraid of everything. I was afraid to have friends. I was afraid to go places. I was afraid just to be myself. I still have struggles with these things, but that is just it. I continue to struggle with these things. I am not allowing them to overtake me.

Do I wish things were different on my journey? Sometimes I do. I wish that the first therapist I saw didn't perpetuate the abuse by touching me. Therapists have a good deal of power over people with mental issues. I wasn't able to defend myself because I was so mentally defeated.

I wish the school therapist had taken the time to listen to my story because everybody's story is different. Even if you felt like you have heard the same story a million times, each story is unique because of the individuals themselves. I was devastated to not be believed, and nobody should have to feel that.

I wish that if a therapist didn't know how to deal with a case like mine, he or she would tell me they couldn't help me. I felt like I wasted a year in therapy trying to do the right thing, but failing.

As the months of therapy continued, Katie began to change from the inside out. She continues to work tirelessly in her sessions. Her persistence is a constant encouragement to me. She has a strong desire to free herself of the chains of her past. With a greater boldness, she considers when and with whom boundaries need to be drawn. Then she decides where the limit is and firmly holds the line.

Considering where she began, her improvement astounds all who hear her story. Katie has found her voice. She speaks decisively for herself. More and more she is able to speak her mind without feeling like she is unworthy of being heard. Her growth inspires me to continue the work of helping with trauma patients. She is a living testimony of the power of persistent endurance. She overcame each and every obstacle in an effort to free herself to be recreated in identity, intimacy, and personality! She survived!

During my work with Katie, it became apparent that two very effective treatment options for her were writing and art. Both of these helped her move past her difficulty in speaking to be able to express herself with alternatives. Once, I asked Katie to draw me a picture of an image that represents her journey through struggle toward freedom, and here's what she drew:

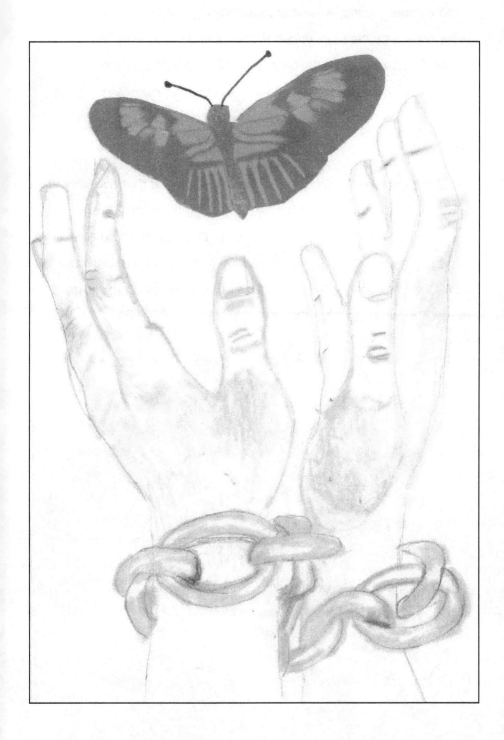

Why did I draw the picture? Well, the easy answer is because you asked me to. You wanted me to draw a picture that represented my story. To me, the book and the picture are both about struggle and transformation. I drew my hands bound by chains because that's what sexual abuse did to me. It made me a prisoner of lies and pain. I took a picture of a butterfly and am reaching for it like I'm grasping for reality, reaching for hope and change.

I want to share one final letter from Katie that will give you a glimpse of where she currently is in her life and where she's going:

So, I want to tell you some things. What better way to do that than by how this all started, with a letter. Before I started counseling with you, I had admitted myself to a mental hospital, because I had nowhere to turn. I had been in and out of therapy for years with several different therapists. They all told me the same thing: They would work with me for a few months, and my issues should be resolved. Between therapy, physical therapy, and several combinations of medications, I was barely surviving. I thought about dying every day.

When I came out of the hospital, I was so confused on not only what I was feeling, but also what I believed in. I guess I didn't understand why I was still suffering but was supposed to forgive the people that caused the suffering. I knew I was supposed to. I just didn't know how. That's when I first talked to you. You said you wanted to help me. I wasn't sure. I didn't think I could be helped, and I didn't want to waste your time. But I couldn't give up. I felt like this was my last chance.

When you read my journal and responded the way you did, I felt hope. When you said you wouldn't give up on me, I believed you. I just wasn't sure there was anything to be done. However, I wanted to do anything to get better because the alternative was pretty much death.

A year ago I was slipping closer and closer towards nothingness. I never told anyone that because, really, what would be the point? Actually, the point of this letter isn't about where I have been or what I have gone through. It's about where I am going.

You saved my life. No matter how silly that sounds, it is the truth. I now have hope and a future. I am crying when I write this, and it's okay. That right there proves that I have changed. I have identifiable feelings. I am able to feel like an actual human and not a mistake.

I used to be more afraid of living than dying. Now, I want to help people who are like me. I want to work on continuing to be better and stronger. I know there is more I have to work on. But, for the first time, I am not scared. I am determined. I have no doubt in my mind where I am going. I also want God to be in my life. I have always been confused about God's role in people's lives. Even though I knew it wasn't His fault, I still secretly blamed Him. I am ashamed I felt this way. I don't think He had anything to do with me being hurt, but He had everything to do with me surviving and starting new.

Anyway, I am sorry this is so long. Just imagine if I talked like I write. Maybe someday I will. The actual point of this letter is to say, "Thank You." Thank you for all those nights you sat with me for hours trying to help me the best you could. You don't know how much I wanted to let you in. I just didn't know how to find the door. I want you to know that I listened to everything you ever said and was fortified by it. I don't think I can adequately express how you changed my life for the better. I will never be the same. I think God put you in my life to help me be free. So, thank you.

All the frustrating, tiring, and endless hours of sitting in silence are worth ever so much when you read where Katie is in her life today. She truly is a changed person. For every person who has suffered sexual trauma, may I say, "Let Katie serve to inspire you to reach out for help." Like her, you may find helpers who are not able to effectively assist you. Keep searching.

In many countries, there are numerous professionals who have the training and desire to help you to become healthier and more fulfilled as a human being. All people deserve lives of respect and honor. Although millions do suffer abuse, it does not mean they are not worthy of being loved. If you are one of those people, let me say to you: You are deserving and worthy of love.

Find the helper best suited for you. Do the difficult work *necessary for becoming a better you. With new perspective, you will eventually become capable of becoming the person you've always wanted to be. Hear Katie's newfound voice urging you on! You can be more. You can become. Reach for the new you and you may find yourself...**Released!***

Call Paul

Dr. Paul Helton is available to speak at your next conference, group, or special event. Please feel free to call and book an event. Also, if you would just like to talk for a couple of minutes regarding questions you might have about recovery, treatment, or EMDR please place a call to his cell number. If there is no answer, please leave a message and allow time for a follow up call.

Paul's Cell Phone Number:

(731) 377-9724